MommyBest:

13 Inspirational Lessons Derek & Dylan's Mom (and maybe yours) Never Learned in School!

Book 1:
Memoirs from the first five years of motherhood.

For Moms of All Ages . . . Everywhere!

Written by Donna Scrima-Black
With the help of her boys, her joys!!

PUBLISHING HOUSE

Visit our website at:
www.mommybestbook.com

Words By Sweetness Publishing House, Inc
P.O. Box 468
Jefferson Valley, NY 10535-0468

Copyright © 2009 by Donna Scrima-Black
All rights reserved.

Library of Congress Control Number 2009924597

ISBN 978-0-9819783-0-7

Dedication

To My Boys, My Joys:

My husband, Kevin, who loved me exactly as I am from the moment he met me.

My son, Derek, the first boy I ever loved—unconditionally—the moment I held him.

My son, Dylan, who taught me motherhood is as wondrous and miraculous the second son around.

To my female cheerleaders for always standing alongside me:

My mother, Lynn;

My twin sister, Deborah;

My best friend, Margi.

To mothers everywhere who share an invisible and invincible "mommy" shield of honor in the sacredness of their mission.

Foreword

In recent years it has been customary to have a famous person write the "Foreword" for a book. I don't happen to fit that mold, however, I like to think I am famous….at least in my own house!

After reading these stories, you will have a better understanding of women and the hard choices they make. Are women of the 90's and the 21st Century supposed to focus on climbing the corporate ladder? Or, are we seeing a retrospective of the woman of the 50's-a woman who stays home to care for the children? I think we're seeing both and a lot more creative scenarios of family life than ever existed before. Contrary to what most recent books say, I don't believe women can have it all. There is no way they can have a worthwhile career, a gratifying family life and a rewarding personal life at the same time. Something has to give as there is only so much time in a day, quality time, that is! The key is to find which one of these choices makes you happiest and build your life from its core.

For all those women (and men) who haven't slept through the night until their child was four years old, and for all those parents who truly know what it takes to raise a child the best way they can, to give him what our parents couldn't, I salute you. There are, of course, some parents in this world who have nine kids (who were lucky enough to have them all sleep through the night) and find life to be grand, while others struggle to parent one. Everyone's idea of "good" parenting is different, so each family needs to define it for themselves.

Donna has been given the gift of writing, yet her true gift is revealed in these passages. When you read through these "lessons," I'm sure you will be apt to reflect on where your life has changed, how it has changed and perhaps you will even see some similarities in your parenting. I find myself almost living on the outside, not believing these events actually transpired, some of them, only years ago.

It is true what my mother and father said—"Life goes by so fast!" My hope when you read these lessons is that you take a moment to just sit back and enjoy what you have, to hopefully learn something about yourself and your children.

I know I am truly blessed to have a beautiful wife, mother and person, to share these once in a lifetime moments. Cherish them and cherish these lessons like I do!

Regards,
Kevin Black

Contents

Foreword	v
Preface	ix
Acknowledgements	xiii
Introduction & How to Use this Book	xix

Lesson 1: The Birth of a Mom
Each Woman's Journey into Motherhood Is Unique!   1

Lesson 2: Playing House Is Fun if You're the C.E.O.
Moving-up the Homemaker Ladder of Success!   15

Lesson 3: Number Two Should Fit like a Shoe!
A Pair of Shoes Is Better than One—
The Second Boy Around.   29

Lesson 4: "Play-dates for Playmates"
Whatever Happened to Making Mud Pies?   41

Lesson 5: Identical Twins
There's More than Meets the Eye When Raising Twins
and Other Siblings—Especially When Twins/Siblings
Become Moms.   51

Lesson 6: My Friend, "Aunt Margi"
"Wild and Crazy" to "Thursday Night Shoppers." 65

Lesson 7: Some Wonderful Things Can Happen if the North Meets the South
My Boys, My Joys: A Tale of Opposites! 81

Lesson 8: Changing Seasons
The Rummage Sale: A Lesson in Letting Go! 93

Lesson 9: Moms Have to Get in the Game Too!
The Making of a Sport's Mom 101

Lesson 10: "Specials" Are AWESOME!
Everything at Home Is Boring. Scheduling Some Fun! 111

Lesson 11: Playing Hide & Seek Is Fun
Finding Mom Can Be the Hard Part Once Kids Leave the Nest to Do Their Kindergarten Best. 119

Lesson 12: Holiday Memories
"Kitty" and Grandmothers. 129

Lesson 13: Evens verses Odds
Having Number Three, Looking For a Girl like Me! 139

Postscript 147

Preface

When I became a mother, my perspective of the world changed in a flash—from the way I thought about some of the "big questions" surrounding the proverbial meaning of life—to the manner in which I approached everyday, mundane tasks that had taken on a whole new meaning; the cooking, cleaning and laundry I now performed had a direct impact on the well being of my children, something that had become sacred to me.

Once our first son, Derek, was born, our world was never the same. My husband and I were filled with so much joy and love for him. Then, in an instant, the joy turned into an overwhelming sense of fear when our son was taken from us due to a head injury he sustained during delivery. I had developed a fever during the last stage of a very long labor, so my obstetrician attached an internal electronic fetal monitor clip to Derek's scalp to check his heart rate. Unfortunately, he forgot to remove the monitor clip from Derek's skull before securing a vacuum extractor to his head prior to delivery. The end result left a gaping hole in his head. The nurses insisted Derek get an x-ray of his injury immediately. Thankfully, no internal damage was seen and no spinal fluid was present.

Still, Derek developed a fever, and a spinal tap had to be performed. I knew it was serious because the attending nurse wouldn't look me in the eye when I asked her if my son was going to be "okay." I later discovered it was because this nurse, also a mom, was trying to mask her own worry, which she later told me would have been conveyed in her eyes and by her facial expressions.

After weeks of hospital care, with my husband and I beside his incubator in the "Special Care Nursery," Derek was able to come home with the pediatrician's seal of good health.

Family, friends and even some hospital staff had suggested we sue the obstetrician for negligence, which we could have done, I believe, and won. Instead, I held so much gratitude our prayers for Derek's recovery were answered; I wanted to surround him with positive energy and all the goodness life has to offer, especially since he already had experienced a rough entry into this world.

As a bona fide career woman my entire life, I always held, deep within my heart, a hidden passion to write. Although I published some of my works, I instead pursued a more lucrative business career, fearful I wouldn't be able to meet my financial obligations. I also think I was scared to fail. Since my dream of becoming a famous author had yet to be realized, I thought a book focusing on empowering other moms, highlighting the beautiful moments of motherhood, would be a fitting way to pay tribute to our family's journey. To that end, this book, *MommyBest: 13 Inspirational Lessons Derek & Dylan's Mom (and maybe yours) Never Learned in School*, was born. The title, *MommyBest...*, represents every mother's efforts to be her best!

I also rationalized money from the book's sales would

go towards my children's education. Once sales surpass my expectations, it is my intent to contribute select amounts to various charities dedicated to helping children and families; some of these organizations I currently support while some have been brought to my attention by other moms I've met who advocate on their behalf. In this way, I feel I am sharing my success, as I ask others to do, with families in need.

I never expected to instinctually transform into a mom; nor could I envision the most amazing part of my world to write about would be my experiences with my children. My mom metamorphosis hit quicker than a fast ball ripped at me, and I instinctively shifted to receive the catch, unaware for the longest time of the impact the ball had on me when it hit. I just approached each day learning and growing along with my baby. There wasn't time for reflection.

I was somewhat more prepared for my second son, but this time the pitch was a curve ball, and again, I automatically adjusted my position to make the catch. It wasn't 'till several months passed I reflected upon the ways in which I had become a very different person, who found herself on a very different playing field: I was a mom—Derek and Dylan's Mom, someone, who-before I had my baby boys, my joys-would never have imagined using baseball comparisons because sports wasn't a big part of my life. I had spent so much time preparing to be a successful, financially secure-maybe even, famous-woman, very skeptical of getting married and/or having children for fear of becoming dependent and losing my identity. Although there are times when I still feel a little lost in my motherhood role, my children have actually guided me to uncover my true self—as well as find a path in life I now realize I was destined to ultimately travel.

I love being Derek and Dylan's Mom as they are the two most wondrous gifts that have ever been bestowed on my husband and I. They have been my precious inspiration, guiding me to again explore my passion to write. I have spent any scattered moments of free time working on this book, excited by the experiences and discovering the underlying meaning in all the glories as well as some of the struggles.

Ultimately, I learned motherhood is not a destination as much as it is a voyage that is always full of surprises because each of us, and our lives, is constantly changing. Creative choices exist today that didn't when my mom was raising her children and there were fewer options, and, therefore, less confusion. The trick for each of us now is to find the unique balance that works to fulfill our individual dreams along with those for our families.

Acknowledgements

Embarking on the journey of motherhood is an amazing adventure filled with lots of excitement and commotion. At times it can be an overwhelming and lonely trip. I was lucky enough to have some women—and a few men—who cheered me on, supporting my transformation and encouraging me to explore my life.

Although the subject of this book is motherhood, I submit that beside (not behind as the cliché for men is) every lucky mom, is a "good" and *luckier* father. On that note, I must honor my copilot—my husband and boys' father—Kevin. He has supported my endeavors as a woman and a wife/mother before it was politically or socially correct to do so. He is our sons' hero, always teaching them about such things as sports—playing and respecting the games—math (he's a much better mathematician than I am), the importance of honoring promises and keeping commitments, working hard to achieve goals, the *value of respecting women*—in short, Life Lessons from a Father's perspective to help our boys become great men—all the while inspiring them to pursue their dreams! Since this book is written from a Mom's perspective, I invited my husband to have the honor of writing the "Foreword" for *MommyBest…* in order to provide our audience with a *FatherBest* insight of the first five years of parenting.

I must also honor my father who, despite our differing philosophies on life, has been there for me, especially during many hardships along the way. He often worked 24-hour shifts to support his family as a lieutenant fireman in the Bronx, NY until retirement. I vividly recall all the times he graciously handed his paycheck to my mom every two weeks to provide for his five children. My dad still reminds me, rearing his somewhat chauvinistic underpinnings, I can do anything because I have "HIS genes."

The next two male heroes I am honored to thank are the smallest in size, yet occupy the biggest space in my heart: my sons, Derek and Dylan, who have reached into the depths of my soul in a way that words can't convey. Suffice to say they help me see all the beauty in the world and especially in my life. They have inspired me to be ME!

The women who have influenced my life must begin with my mother who has always unconditionally loved me, and once I formed my own family, she has bestowed her love upon them. She is one of the kindest, most giving women I know. Although we are different in many ways, we are bonded in our role as mothers and the sacredness of raising children. My mom always calls me, at least twice a day, to discuss everything and anything, especially issues concerning my boys— her grandchildren. My husband and children joke each time the phone rings that "it's Granny Lynn." I must confess I don't know what I'll do when one inevitable day, down the road (I hope it's a long one), my phone stops ringing and our conversations cease!

Another major cheerleader in my life is my twin sister,

Deborah; we have gone from wearing diapers to changing our children's diapers together, so it doesn't get any closer than that! I respect and admire her as an ambitious, hard working person who is also a devoted and inspirational mother. She has traveled through life with me and has been a godsend, always listening, giving me encouragement and some advice—sometimes when I'm not ready to hear it. It's such a blessing to have a sister and best friend who I implicitly trust to discuss everything from our childhood times together to those of our children's.

My best friend Margi has been another supporter in my life. I have known Margi since sixth-grade, so whenever we get together, it's as if we are school girls getting into mischief. Our lives have taken opposite directions, yet our friendship still evolves and grows stronger. Margi is one of the most independent women I know; she is comfortable with herself and being by herself. She has always encouraged me in all my aspirations and lifts my spirits when I'm down.

All three women in my life have cheered me on to write. They are my fans as they read my stories and applaud my efforts. It is thanks to them—and my husband and children—I dare to follow my dream of publishing a book containing these shared experiences and teachings.

There are also hundreds of people I've become friendly with or casually meet who have encouraged me in any and every way possible, including: other moms; women I meet at the supermarket I shop, businesses I frequent, restaurants where I indulge myself, and even the waiting room at the doctor's office. I've tried to use their positive energy to add fuel to my engine.

I invested many, many months waiting for publishers to respond to *MommyBest*. I received several "interested parties" and a few publishing "possibilities" that, in the end, simply did not work out. Frustrated, I contacted a professional business organization comprised of volunteers who help new entrepreneurs, recommended by one of the "how to publish" books. A successful retired businessman immediately returned my call; he was eager to share his suggestions and move this project forward. No one prior to him had ever been so helpful. He had a contact at one of the "Big" publishing houses and personally met with her to share my manuscript. To say that I waited with baited breath to hear from him is an understatement. He e-mailed me the comment from the female editor which read: *MommyBest*....was "sweet, but ordinary."

Given the uphill struggle in the publishing industry, he advised I shouldn't "waste" my time trying to publish this book as the task and likelihood of making any money was comparable to someone becoming a "rock star."

When I first read his e-mail, I literally felt a pang pressing from my insides. I wondered why, when I finally thought I could be on the road to success, I was again disappointed. In an instant my mind flashed back to an unpleasant college experience: One of my journalism professors, known for spewing disapproving comments, condescendingly rolled his eyes before advising me I had "some" (in a tone synonymous with "not much") writing talent. My belly ached that day too, before I took action.

I pushed the pangs from the inside of my belly outward by taking several deep breaths. Soon I was smiling, remembering my professor's condescending remarks prodded me to prove him wrong. Within a few months of hearing his remarks, I had my first magazine article published. So, maybe this businessman's recommendation was put in my path as a force to again prompt me to move forward. I responded via e-mail with:

"Thank you for your candor and all the help you have given me. I wish you and your family wonderful things in your future."

With that in mind, I must also thank those in my life who have doubted me and my determination to make my dream come true. All your nay says have brought higher graces and more "yes's" into my life!

I felt as if I didn't have a choice in this endeavor. I *had t*o publish my "ordinary" story. Ironically, as a mom, I ultimately discovered so much of the beauty in motherhood is seeing the *extraordinary* in the ordinary; my entire life experience up to becoming "Mom" was a prelude for me to understand: often, the most complex is found in the simple, everyday mundane tasks in life. As shared in the play, *Our Town,* by Arthur Miller, the character Emily, who has died after giving birth, is given an opportunity to visit any day of her life. She wants to return to a "happy day" that's somewhat "ordinary," her 12th birthday. When she discovers her family obliviously performing everyday tasks, Emily questions why the "Living," don't recognize how lucky they are. She concludes "they" (people living) don't understand the beauty in their everyday lives.

In my effort to seize the day, it has taken me over 10 years to put my thoughts to paper in a way I am proud of and believe moms can relate to. *I* wanted to publish my book—our stories—myself and have control over the finished work. I didn't want to sensationalize the text. I'm seeking truth in my own life, so why would I share anything less with my audience?

Introduction & How to Use this Book

Since there is such a barrage of instructional/"how to" parenting materials abound, I, instead use a book format that first shares a brief summary for each lesson, followed by the personal story associated with it. The book is a quick, hopefully spirited read, CliffsNotes, if you will, weaving together some motherhood pragmatics with poignant, empowering memoirs.

With the help of my children's wisdom, I wrote this book as a way to share some of the MOMMY LIFE LESSONS I have learned during the first five years of being a mother.

Topics woven into my lessons include:

- changes women undergo on their journey into motherhood
- making personal and creative choices for balancing career and home
- preparing for a second child

- finding suitable "play dates" for mom and baby
- nurturing relationships with one's own mom, siblings and close friends
- learning to trust maternal instinct with issues such as choosing the "appropriate" nursery school
- living with "opposite" children
- becoming a child's number-one "fan"
- coping with children growing-up so quickly
- helping children have excitement in play
- cherishing children's relationship with "Grandma"
- caring for "Mommy" and her dreams
- creating lasting familial memories while continuing to grow as a mom and *a woman.*

It's my hope readers will connect with my experiences and be moved to reflect upon their own journeys. To that end, I have included a "Reader Reflection" page after each memoir. It would be silly of me to expect readers to solely interpret my experiences without hoping to, in some way, speak to their own lives. Plus, the "teacher" in me always encourages my students, as well as myself, to jot down any responses to written material, whether they're observations, questions, wonders or even drawings. I encourage women to read the book in any order they choose, as each memoir deals with a separate topic as part of the entire collection of lessons about motherhood. So, if a special topic or title speaks to them, they can go to that lesson and discover their own voice.

In this way, ***MommyBest...*** can be used as a springboard for each woman to compile her own collection of life experiences, and as I use to say to my students, make "self to text connections." I've even included a few questions or "wonderings" at the bottom of each "Reader Reflection" page as a prompt.

Unlike me, some moms are able to write down their children's daily milestones. In the hustle and bustle of each day, I only recorded a few verbatim. Instead, I later pondered upon the day, week or whichever time period or accomplishment and its significance to me and/or our family life. Depending upon personal preference, each individual may use the "Reader Reflection" page as a forum for recording household happenings, however specific or general in nature they are. It is a place for readers to sow the seeds for their family memoir: a living recording they will enhance as they and their lives evolve along with their loved ones.

Today, more than ever, women need to rally together because, unlike "olden times" when moms had relatives and neighborly friends close by, we are often isolated and bombarded by an overload of career and domestic choices to make and responsibilities to take on. We need a network of support—girlfriends to rely on when things become overwhelming and we simply need to have a good talk or go out for some fun!

Since I've become a mom, I have met countless other mothers who have confided they too have struggled with the complex range of emotions and situations I, and many families, face. I even provided some of these moms with a copy of one of my stories—whichever anecdote was relevant at the moment—to read. Much to my surprise and delight, those moms graciously confessed they felt as if I was writing about "their" lives and were happy someone was coming "out of the kitchen" to validate the vital—and yet often undervalued—accomplishments of moms.

It is my intent that *MommyBest…* will leave an imprint on the readers' minds so they will reflect/assess/adjust their own choices and the consequence of each in helping to create a happy and balanced life; to encourage women to surround themselves with a network of people who will support the difficult decisions we make; to cherish becoming a mother and choose the family/career life that each of us so desire; and finally—and possibly the most significant—is to help create a universal paradigm shift of our cultural view of women so our society, in its entirety, pays homage to all mothers for their daily contributions and sacrifices on behalf of their children's and family's well being. Motherhood, at the very least, should be recognized and receive the venerable status CEOs and other so-called "leaders" at the helm enjoy—who don't even have to "do diapers." What else is nobler than devoting oneself to nurturing and developing children's lives and the future of our world?

In closing, I must honor and thank God for his encouragement, devotion and unwavering love throughout my journey in Life! Additionally, as a mom with two sons, I must also express my gratitude to Mary, the Mother of God, who I often seek guidance from. Mary, according to my beliefs, displayed to the world the incomprehensible and absolute strength of a mother's unconditional love with the ultimate sacrifice she made.

MommyBest:

13 Inspirational Lessons Derek & Dylan's Mom (and maybe yours) Never Learned in School!

Book 1:
Memoirs from the first five years of motherhood

For Moms of All Ages . . . Everywhere!

Written by Donna Scrima-Black
With the help of her boys, her joys!!

LESSON 1

The Birth of a Mom—
Each Woman's Journey into Motherhood Is Unique!

Once I had my own child, I finally understood the greatness of my own mother's unconditional love and devotion to her children.

Decisions about whether or not to seek marriage and family are rooted in our own childhood family experiences. Contrary to my mother's dreams of getting married and raising children, I dreamt of financial independence and a successful career. The philosophy of the Woman's Movement influenced me greatly in seeking to achieve my goals, never really differentiating them from my *dreams*.

Throughout my growing years, I never understood the joy and utter fulfillment my own mother derived from raising her five children, and I often questioned what her personal longings were.

During my pregnancy I began a transformative journey. Yet, it wasn't until I delivered my son that I *knew* I was a *different* person.

From the moment I held my son, I felt a bond like no other before—a bond that reached into the depths of my soul, beyond expression, beyond comprehension.

I realized along with a baby—a mom had been born—and a deeper union with my own mother was formed. I knew I had always been destined to become a mother. I just had to navigate my own journey—in my own time, and in my own way!!

So, to all the women readers of this book and those who honor them:
If you are meant to be a mother, you will be one—in your own way and in your own time!!!!!!!!!!!!!!!!!!!!!!!!!!

The Birth of a Mother—
Each Woman's Journey into Motherhood Is Unique.

Ever since I was a little girl, I had big dreams. I would spend hours each day listening to my radio imagining how all my dreams would come true. As the music played, my heart raced as I saw myself traveling to far away places, becoming famous and rich, and most importantly—emerging as an independent woman.

Sometimes, before bedtime, I would share my dreams with my mother who always listened with eager and excited ears. All my dreams were a stark contrast to my mom's childhood dream of getting married and raising children. I couldn't understand, given all the opportunities I had, how my mother could derive such pleasure and fulfillment from motherhood. And, since I knew all about life, so I thought, I often advised my mom to do "more" with hers,' besides "just being a mother."

As I grew and went to school, I often watched my mother throughout the day. With her eyes half-opened and what we would describe today as a really "bad hair day," she would scurry in the morning to prepare breakfast for her five children, pack our lunches, find lost items we were distraught about and mediate our arguments, not to mention the house cleaning and chauffeuring she constantly did. Mom repeated her mother's dance of caring for everyone else's needs throughout the day—two steps here, two steps there. I was determined not to follow her lead, especially after she had to be hospitalized several times due to a medical condition, related to exhaustion. As a youngster, unable to fully understand my mom's bouts of exhaustion, I struggled blaming myself and even her for the times she was absent when I needed her.

So, each evening while I listened to my music, I orchestrated the course of my life—and becoming a mom was not part of my score. Instead, I imagined traveling to far away places while becoming a famous movie star or a powerful businesswoman.

I studied and practiced my entrepreneurial skills early on by charging my siblings a few cents for cooking such delicious breakfast meals as mayonnaise sandwiches. I often babysat for the younger children in the neighborhood who I loved to boss around. Sometimes, I'd even help my brother deliver newspapers, especially on Sundays when I could browse through all the fashion magazines before shopping. Often, the persuasive headlines lured me into reading many of the amazing stories. The words, like music, stirred my emotions long after they were read and lingered like flavors savored after a delicious meal. I was compelled to add becoming a famous writer to my collection of dreams, a collection I examined, revised, admired and cherished in my mind each time I listened to the lyrics and rhythm of my favorite melodies.

My entrepreneurial skills strengthened as I finished high school and went on to college, continuing to work after school and waitress some nights and weekends. During my junior year, it was difficult to select a major; I vacillated as to which career to pursue, and with so many choices, like items on a menu, I wanted to try them all.

Then, during my junior year, I saw an ad in the campus newspaper seeking Staff Reporters. With nervous excitement, I applied and was given the opportunity to cover the events affecting campus life. Each story that I covered, like parts of my life, had different pieces to fit together. I agonized for hours piecing my words together like a quilt. The first time I saw my name flashing above my words, I felt dizzy with a sense of accomplishment. So when I listened to my music, I felt as if shots of adrenalin were traveling throughout my veins at the thought of becoming a writer.

As time went on, a few professors persuaded me, given my enthusiasm to become "independent," to seek a more financially rewarding career. I followed their advice and decided to pursue a career in advertising.

Still, I loved the attention my stories received from other students and faculty alike. I also felt important interviewing and reporting on the school's major social events, and especially enjoyed receiving recognition from my boyfriend of three years and his teammates at their soccer games. Unfortunately, by my senior year, I knew that my boyfriend wanted a "traditional" wife instead of someone who wanted to explore her options, as I did.

So, as many of my friends graduated college and moved out on their own pursuing their careers and/or marriage, I returned to my parent's home—unable to find my coveted advertising job and not really sure which direction to turn. All my other siblings moved out of "the nest" and my dad was still working full time plus extra hours.

I began to spend time with my mom, the one person I had really drifted apart from during my rebellious teenage years. At first, it was awkward connecting with her. We talked many nights about how I felt when, during my growing years, she had been sick several times and away from the family. It was painfully obvious that she was devastated recalling the times when she was recovering in the hospital. Now mature, I was finally able to better understand how exhausted my mom was having five children—one right after the other, including twins. She did the best she could under some very stressful conditions. From our discussion and some tears, we were able to move to a deeper relationship. We started having late night talks again as we had when I was younger; but now it felt as if we were girlfriends sharing our secrets. She became my cheerleader, always excited about what was going on in my life.

After countless interviews and several "in-between" jobs, an advertising company hired me as a Sales Representative; Ecstatic about my opportunity, Mom shopped for days with me for a new wardrobe. As she scavenged through the racks of clothes, I reminisced about all our shopping trips we went on while I was growing up. Each year before school started, Mom would take my sisters and I to the department stores to buy five new outfits, one for each day of the school week. And she would buy us "only the best of shoes" because she didn't want us to become "flat-footed."

Yet, Mom rarely bought any clothes for herself or for my father, a New York City firefighter who often worked

24-hour shifts, always graciously handing most of his earnings to Mom each week. As I watched him place money into her hand, I made a conscious decision to strive to become fiscally self-reliant.

Although my parents financially struggled, neither of them ever complained about their lack of material things, or for the amount of money they spent on us. Sometimes, during the holiday season, my mother's favorite time of the year, my parents would secure a bank loan so we could have a lot of the things "they never had as kids." Even though we were far from rich, friends who saw our clothes and bicycles, for example, thought we were.

Once I started my new job, I began to feel like a kid again. Mom would have dinner and her listening ears waiting when I got home. She wanted to know all about my day: the people I met; the sales I made; and the places I visited. I knew Mom was vicariously living some of my experiences; I enjoyed all the attention. When I had enough money to buy a place of my own, it was difficult to leave.

So, in preparation of my independence—and for a much needed break from working days and evenings, making sales quotas and meeting deadlines—I planned the European trip I dreamt of as a little girl watching movies of women traveling abroad, often discovering themselves and romance.

Even though my mom, like me, is petrified to fly, she offered to accompany me on my journey. I knew I had to go alone. I booked the trip as part of a tour group so I would have some direction and companionship. Days before my scheduled departure, I listened for hours to my favorite Italian songs, including "Three Coins in a Fountain" and "Volare."

Although I was advised to travel "light," I spent days before my trip shopping with my mom.

When the departure time came, I was petrified. There was a lot of turbulence during the beginning of the flight, but the ride became calmer, as did I.

It wasn't long before I was standing in Saint Mark's Square in Venice with pigeons adorning my head and shoulders. When I sat down for a cup of cappuccino, I was part of a magnificent audience serenaded by string instruments. As I listened to the music, my own heartstrings were strummed. I remembered how I longed for this moment since I was a little girl listening to music and dreaming of traveling to far away places—except now those places were near.

As my soul soared, a waiter graciously placed a complimentary cup of cappuccino in front of me. An admirer sitting nearby had ordered it. I raised my head and looked for the wealthy European I dreamt of meeting. A young man stood before me. He was an American tourist who, ironically, thought I was European. There were no romantic sparks, but I had met a friend. We shared some highlights from our trip with each other before I returned to my hotel to prepare for the scheduled gondolier ride with my tour group.

Under the glow of the moon, the other tourists and I boarded the gondolier. We were all relaxed sitting beside the glistening waters as we were serenaded. I felt vitalized and tranquil at the same time. I also had the feeling someone was staring at me; it was the same feeling I had for much of the tour, but I was too busy to acknowledge it. But this night, the watchful gaze—against the starlight and music—was recognized. The azure eyes did belong to a European this time. Still, he wasn't the rich man I dreamt about either. The admirer was our tour bus driver. Even though he spoke only a few words of English, we spent the remainder of my stay together. As the bus driver resided in Rome, he gave me a personal tour of all the sights, ending with the Trevi Fountain, which, ironically, was under construction, as I felt I had been.

I threw many coins in and made many wishes—as well as expressions of gratitude for the experiences I shared with some wonderful people, especially the bus driver from Rome! Needless to say, weeks passed as if they were only days and my departure came. It was difficult boarding the plane, saying goodbye to my European adventure and my personal tour guide.

Like a kid looking in a candy store window, Mom was waiting at the airport for me. Her eyes scoped the crowd at the arrival gate. "Donna, Donna," she screamed! "You're glowing." I was aglow! Weeks after my trip, coworkers continued to tell me that I looked different. I felt different.

Without realizing it, I was ready to journey within and see my life anew. Once I listened to my inner voice, the one that's connected to my heart and guides me to joyful places, my life, like dominoes, began to fall into place.

Soon, I moved out of my childhood home and purchased a two-bedroom condominium. My mom and I were very emotional on moving day, but we both understood the closeness we established would always be near, even when we are apart.

Filled with so much vitality and excitement, I pursued my career, working well into the evenings. One night while working late, a new sales representative called the office for his messages. I answered and we talked for over two hours. He asked if he could see the photos I had taken in Europe. I obliged.

For our date, he arrived with a single white rose. We went to a restaurant similar to the ones I had visited in Europe—filled with the aroma of freshly ground coffee beans. The cozy, round tables were covered with paper; each table had a container filled with crayons. After several hours of conversation, accompanied by scrumptious food, we sipped our cappuccinos while viewing the photos. My date asked me to use one of the crayons to make a list of the important qualities I want in a husband and he would do the same for a wife. Amazingly, when we compared our lists, they were almost identical.

With paper in hand, we went for a drive to a nearby park for a brisk walk. I was given a piggyback ride through a beautifully wooded forest where a white-tailed deer leaped out in front of us just as my date kissed me. Without speaking, we looked at each other knowing this deer was somehow symbolic, even magical.

That evening when I listened to my music, I thought about the romance I sought on my European vacation, around the world. Then, practically in my own backyard, I met the man of "my dreams." In contrast with my lavish trip, my date and I were in a park filled with greenery and the beauty of nature and its amazing creatures. The clusters of trees, all leading to different paths seemed to hold many surprises and many hopes.

One surprise was finding myself back at school pursuing a Master's Degree in Education. Teaching, a profession women stereotypically work at, was not the occupation I dreamt about as a young businesswoman. Yet, it was a profession I now felt would allow me to contribute more to the world on behalf of children. I soon learned my students often taught me lessons about life. It's amazing how intelligent and genuine they are. They became my family with whom I shared much of my life with.

When I accepted a marriage proposal from the man who kissed me in the park, my students were so happy, as was my mother. My mom understood I wasn't like several of my friends who began planning for their weddings when they were teenagers. I never dreamt of getting married. And the men who I had thought I might possible wed one day, soon wanted me to change myself, in some way—whether it was to sacrifice my career aspirations or distance myself from my girlfriends. Now I had met someone who loved me *exactly* the way I was and supported my goals—whatever they were. Some call it kismet, others destiny?

I soon learned why some women start early in life planning their weddings. I discovered it was exciting yet exhausting planning for "the Big Day." The entire event was surreal until I found myself walking down the aisle. As I moved forward I walked along a path, viewing as I would a movie, many of the important people in my life, including some of my students, to the altar where my husband-to-be waited for us to embark on our journey.

The following year, we decided to start a family and instantly everything just "fell into place:" My husband and I were having a baby! Unlike many of my previous business decisions I often contemplated, analyzing lots of information, I simply followed my instincts; it felt "right". The news prompted my students to plan a surprise shower for me. I couldn't believe (nor could my mother) I was going to be a mom. Since I was absolutely positive I would be having a girl, it was the biggest surprise of my life when I gave birth to a son.

The instant I held him, I felt a bond like no other—a bond that reached into the depths of my soul, beyond expression, beyond comprehension. I realized along with a baby, a mother had been born—a parent was in the making.

As I looked into my son's innocent eyes, I knew I had always been destined to become a mother, even though I hadn't been ready to acknowledge this while I was achieving all the goals I was determined to accomplish. I was too scared of losing my own identity and too busy proving I was someone "more" and something "else."

Although I had taken a different road than the one my mother followed toward motherhood, I realized we both arrived at our destinations on time—the time that was right for each of us. We are two women, similar in some ways and different in others, somewhat products of the eras that we grew-up in, somewhat products of our unique personas.

Now, as I listen to my music, my heart soars as I dream dreams for my son:

Who will he become? What will he enjoy doing? Which paths will he follow? How shall I guide him? How will he guide me?

As his mother, I am embarking upon an amazing journey—like no other journey I've been on—one toward true self-discovery! I begin this journey with a deep love, gratitude and respect for one who has traveled through the precarious terrain and rough waters of motherhood before me, my own mother. I understand her sacrifice and love—and now perceive her as a woman of greatness for all she has given to her children.

I also recognize I am becoming more of an independent person by pursuing my dreams—as my son has helped me to find a new voice in my writing. I must bring to him the best person I can be first, and then I'll be the best Mommy to him—when my choices reflect who I am at any given moment in my life. No matter which direction my path turns, I am a mother. I am Derek's Mom—now and forever!

Reader Reflection

- How did you arrive (or plan to) at motherhood?
- What do you want to share about this journey for your child(ren) to one day learn?

_____
_____
_____
_____
_____
_____
_____
_____
_____
_____
_____
_____
_____
_____
_____
_____
_____
_____
_____
_____
_____
_____
_____
_____
_____

LESSON 2:

Playing House Is Fun if You're the C.E.O.—

Moving-up the Homemaker Ladder of Success!

As a mom you are immediately promoted to the C.E.O. of your family. In exchange for a business plan, you'll be following a different set of guidelines orchestrating your Life Plan—preparing for your greatest investment ever: your child. It can be a beautiful view once you get to "THE TOP."

When I became Derek's "Mommy," my view on life dramatically changed as my perspective shifted from "Me" to "My Son." It took time for me to finally learn, despite all my career aspirations and the time I invested in achieving them, taking care of my son, was of Greatest Value to me—as was creating internal, home and family harmony. Discovering motherhood opened my heart in new ways which led me to uncover my true self and explore other unexpected passions in my life.

To all my readers, recognize that whether you return to your career, become a full-time mom, or a combination of the two, there's no right or wrong way if you genuinely care for your child. It's critical to FOLLOW YOUR HEART IN MAKING THE DECISION!!!!!!!!!!!!!!!!

Playing House Can Be Fun if You're the CEO!
Moving-up the Homemaker Ladder of Success!

The second I held my newborn son, the life I had so meticulously orchestrated went awry. My carefully laid plans of returning to my job exactly eight weeks after my delivery now seemed insane.

Since I had worked so hard to build my career, I was confident that, although my life would change to some degree when my son was born, it would remain relatively in tact. I wish someone had shared the following insights with me—designed for self-proclaimed career women who are ready to have children, and still determined to "do" and "have it all," as if such a state even exists!

As a new mom, recognize you are now promoted to C.E.O. of your family. But as a C.E.O., you now have a baby on "The Board," so your "business plan" for the greatest investment in your life is a modified version, drastically different than you would have imagined; the following guidelines and anecdotes are from our family's first experiences and the lessons we learned:

> No one can ever fully explain in words the intense love and complex range of emotions you will feel when you give birth to or meet (as in adoption) your child for the very first time. In our case we faced an immediate challenge with the health of our son which caused me to realize the enormity of the love I already felt the instant I met him.

A woman can't even imagine the overpowering flow of emotions she will feel once she has a child; before holding my son, Derek, I had labored for over 30 hours and developed a fever. I was exhausted and somewhat incoherent. Yet, the instant I heard Derek's cries, I became alert—filled with a sense of love and warmth. My heart ached as I wanted to comfort him.

As soon as the nurses placed him in my arms, I felt as if we were always connected—each of us part of a larger being; by some mystery Derek seemed to reach, as no one before ever had, into an untouched part of my soul. When I soothingly kissed his cheek as I said his name, he immediately stopped crying, looked toward my face—recognizing his mother's voice. My husband and I told him how happy we were to have him as our son and how much we loved him.

My joy turned to deep sorrow when Derek had to be taken to the "Special Care Nursery" soon after he was born because he had developed a fever and some other complications as a result of an injury to his head during the birthing process. The obstetrician forgot to remove the fetal monitor clip attached to Derek's head (as I discuss in my "Introduction") before he used the vacuum extraction method of delivery. Unfortunately, my regular obstetrician had to move to a new practice a few weeks before my due date. I hadn't felt comfortable with the new obstetrician from the moment I met him and I should have asked for a different one. Luckily, I was able to hold onto several nurses who I adored and who adored me and Derek from the start. As I reviewed my delivery over and over again in my head during those sleepless nights, I worried and scolded myself for second guessing my intuition; I promised myself I would trust my mommy instincts from then on to watch over Derek.

It's difficult to find the words to describe the anguish I felt when the nurses took my son from my arms. In exchange, I was given a cold, inanimate pen so I could sign a consent form in order for medical tests to be performed—including a Spinal Tap, a test I was told could be very painful. There was a section on the form that read, "Relationship to Patient." Through my tears, I wrote, **for the very first time, the word—"*Mother.*"**

At that moment, I knew becoming a mother was a profound part of my journey in life, a journey that would be filled with intense emotions, including the deep physical and emotional hurt I felt knowing my own son was in pain. I literally felt sick in my heart while he was away—weakened as if someone had knocked the wind out of me.

The days following Derek's birth are a blurred string of events. I don't remember much besides waiting to hear news from the doctors, praying, constantly visiting—and when possible—breastfeeding Derek while checking with the nurses on his progress. I recall frantically asking one nurse if my son was going to be "okay?" When she perfunctorily replied, "I don't know, just relax," as she coldly hooked more wires to his tiny feet, I requested a new nurse. Following my vow to trust my instincts, I made sure the nurses who ultimately tended to him were amazingly loving, tender and caring towards Derek and towards us.

Family, friends and doctors kept telling my husband and I we were handling the situation "so well." Privately we ached and wept, promising each other that we'd keep moving forward so everything would be alright, despite the images of our tiny son—smothered by wires that were connected to huge, engulfing machines. It's a memory that I wish could be erased from my thoughts.

What I vividly recall is feeling as if my husband and I, along with the hospital staff, were actors following the script from a heartbreaking movie. I questioned, "How could this be happening to *us?*" I was determined to rewrite the script with a happy ending. The world, as I had known it before my son's injury, seemed to be somewhere in a far away place.

Although it was difficult to suppress the anger we had, which was constantly justified by the many people who were encouraging us to "sue the doctor," my husband and I made a pact that we would instead concentrate on Derek's healing and pray for his recovery. We focused on allowing ourselves to feel the joy we experienced when the nurses brought him to us for feedings, cuddling and loving. We imagined the beautiful family life we would have in our future.

Through much of our worry we did the best we could

to remain optimistic despite so much uncertainty. After several days—which truly seemed like years in passing—our son's fever miraculously came down and he was on the mend. It was God's *Miracle!*

We were elated when Derek "healed" and was able to come home to spend Thanksgiving, followed by his first Christmas with us. What a gift!!!

> **Transitioning from your career to motherhood takes time and some adjustments.**

During the first few months of staying at home with my son, I was in overdrive. I set tangible goals including reading several books a day to him, in order to feel as if I was accomplishing some measurable level of success, as I had at my job. Although others were urging me to rest when my baby slept, I continued to run on autopilot, still programmed from trying to move-up the so called "career-ladder" during much of my life and trying to transfer that mindset to my motherhood role: I tried to prepare creative meals; play with my son; clean the house; and, study tons from the slew of articles and books I had gathered—each offering help in perfecting my mothering skills. I was even baking homemade cookies for colleagues who visited. I was exhausted doing so much—along with trying to master breastfeeding and tending to my son.

Since I was familiar with my duties throughout my career, I knew how to allocate my time to coordinate and complete projects. In contrast, I felt completely scattered as a homemaker. There was no job description to follow. I didn't receive a paycheck or accolades from my boss or coworkers for my achievements. There were no power lunches or coffee breaks. In fact, I didn't know when to eat lunch and had little, if any, time for social interaction.

I vividly recall one of my husband's colleagues mistakenly calling him on our home phone, instead of at his office. I talked with his associate—God bless his soul—for more than an hour about anything and everything; I was literally starving for conversation and, I guess, some sort of outside connection to the world. I was also seeking some type of validation, maybe someone to tell me I was doing "a good job." Although my twin sister and mother assured me I was, it took me a while to trust this belief, and I continue to second guess myself till this day..

As I began to settle into my motherhood role, I learned instead of getting a big salary with bonuses and vacations, a mother receives big smiles, hugs, kisses and a chance to see the world from her child's wondrous eyes—to experience the newness of life with the wisdom only age brings. Plus, there is someone who, for the first time in your life, truly thinks you are the most amazing person in the world as he searches for you, calls to you, grows with and transforms you. It took time for me to realize, and I still have to remind myself at times, to simply enjoy my son and bask in our time together and at the many intangible feats that are going on.

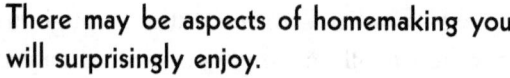

There may be aspects of homemaking you will surprisingly enjoy.

Once I became more comfortable being a mom, it was important for me to make our house a home. When I lived by myself in a condo, I wanted a lavish décor: I had designer window treatments professionally mounted, an updated stereo sound system displayed and a stylish hard wood floor installed.

In complete contrast, I discovered I enjoyed creating an environment that reflects our family's personality. There are play areas for children to feel safe to explore, as well as serene niches to relax so our guests, including "little ones," feel at home. The walls are backdrops for family photos, lots of Derek's masterpieces—plus, homemade quilts, keepsakes and gifts that were made for our family.

If any free time comes my way (which is a rarity), I sometimes try new recipes, or a craft project such as stenciling different sections of our kitchen, or write, my true passion for expression. Naturally, my writing now mirrors my experiences as a mother and, in part, intrinsically speaks from the voice of my son.

I also enjoy being able to plan fun days, which often requires organizational as well as managerial skills—and some creative orchestrating. I feel such a sense of well being when my son has a good night's sleep, when he reaches a milestone as when he learned how to drink from his "sippy" cup instead of his bottle, or when his pediatrician tells me, "Derek is growing beautifully."

I am joyful when my son laughs with another baby on our outings to the park or visits with family and close friends. When we go shopping, this bona fide clotheshorse, whose family has always described her as "glamorous," now delights in dressing the new man in her life. Since we are on a budget, I haven't purchased any new clothes for myself, and am not worried about updating my wardrobe, especially since it's been challenging to get the "last 20" pounds off.

During a recent visit to the pediatrician, we were placed in one of the waiting rooms while the busy doctors tended to their little patients. As I held my tired son, who was awake most of the night due to a vicious ear infection, I glanced at an unrecognizable reflection from the full-length mirror across from us: A worried and tired-looking woman in desperate need of a hair-cut stared back. The grey sweats she wore pinched a little where some extra pounds around her thighs lingered; her heels of yesteryears were replaced with flat sneakers. Instead of a designer pocketbook, she had an over-stuffed diaper bag dangling from her shoulder. I was so shocked that it took me a few moments to mentally process this image was ME!

Yet, as I turned to expose the precious package I held in my arms, my entire perspective changed. I didn't even notice my reflection any more. Instead I saw my son's beautiful face and felt my own beauty from within warmly emerge at the sight of his smile. I felt content he would be feeling better soon, and I, as his mother, would have the honor of tending to him—and to me in due time.

> **You need to recognize that others, especially those who don't have children, may have a difficult time accepting or understanding the changes you have undergone as a result of becoming a mother.**

My family and good friends, who visited me both at the hospital and then at our home, celebrated my new motherhood role along with the emerging perspective I was forming of my life and its direction. In short, they complimented the mom I was becoming. Interestingly, I experienced a different reaction when other acquaintances recently "stopped-by." Some of them innocuously asked me questions that I may have innocently asked other mothers at an earlier stage in my life; questions such as, "What do you do all day," or "Don't you miss working?" Sometimes, in response, I simply laughed recognizing it is only possible to truly appreciate the art and skill of motherhood when you have your own children.

During another visit from a few of the teachers I worked with, only one had a child herself. She was the one who brought me a turkey club sandwich because, as she told me, "You probably skipped lunch so you could clean your house before we got here and get Derek ready for our visit." We hugged each other in kinship.

At a fourth of July celebration with a mix of friends and acquaintances, I remember proudly carrying a cake I decorated before placing it in the center of the table. Most of my friends were cheering my efforts and ogling the dessert. One of our guests, however, snickered, "She's become a regular Martha Stuart." I recognized something about my transformation made her uncomfortable, maybe even jealous.

I soon learned that many women, some of whom I had known for a long time, while others I had only recently met, were fiercely opinionated about the state of motherhood and rules that should accompany it. Some feel women who take a break from their career to rear their children abandon themselves, and, to some degree, insult the efforts of the "Women's Movement;" other women argue motherhood should take priority over all else. Surprisingly, I encountered little understanding and support among many of the women themselves for the different perspectives they held.

I realize mothers today are torn is so many directions and have so many more choices than our mothers had. It is to the credit, in part, of the "Women's Movement" that we do have more opportunities and more options. Yet, what we have gained in options, I believe, we have lost in support: we need to validate all choices and create networks of support and acceptance for the difficult decisions we make, recognizing that each family situation is unique—as each choice is. I also think it's easier to angrily disagree with women who make a different choice because, as women, we may be second guessing our own family decisions, often pressured by financial burdens and stereotyped caricatures of women "having it all."

All of us have to listen to our inner voice of wisdom in order to discover which option or combination thereof provides the key to unlock our destiny, the one providing a balance of joy and fulfillment!

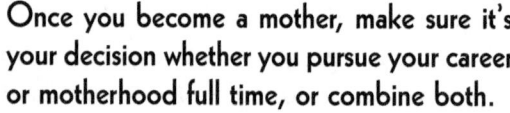

> Once you become a mother, make sure it's your decision whether you pursue your career or motherhood full time, or combine both.

After staying at home with my son for ten months, due to the financial reality of purchasing a new home shortly before his birth, I had to return to my career and place Derek into daycare. We chose what we considered the best daycare, after visiting many, because it had the added benefit of being located next door to my husband's office. My husband and I loved the idea that he could visit our son throughout the day. It was, however, heartbreaking for me to pack Derek up each morning and wave goodbye through my tears. I worried about him so much as I struggled to do my job. My life became so chaotic that neither my work nor my son was getting the best part of me, and I wasn't happy.

There were people in my life who were urging me to "hold on" to my career, while others were warning me that I shouldn't "abandon" my baby.

I had to get quiet enough to listen to my inner voice after asking, "What is most important for my family and for me?"

While I was listening to a sermon at church—praying for guidance—one line resonated with me long after the priest shared it:

"Never trade something of greater value for something of lesser value."

At this time in my life, spending time with my family and discovering myself is of greatest value for me. I also recognize I am a woman who will continue to develop herself and explore her passions in life, including finding creative ways to earn money such as freelance writing. It is only from this continual growth that I can be the best mother to my son and the best person to myself.

When I gave birth to my son, my father said, "From this instant on, your life will never be the same again."

Wonderfully, magically, it hasn't!!

Reader Reflection

- What type of changes have you experienced in your new motherhood role?
- How have those in your life embraced these changes?

LESSON 3

Number Two Should Fit like a Shoe!

A Pair of Shoes Is Better than One—The Second Boy Around.

Unlike our first planned pregnancy, we were happily shocked by the surprise of our second.

I soon discovered that a sibling is the greatest gift we gave each of our children. I was so much more empowered in trusting my mother's instinct as a guide in making decisions for our second son and our family's well being. In that way alone, we could relax more, knowing some of the journey was already paved by our first child's birth and growth.

Our second son is a unique and wondrous boy, an amazing joy for us and his brother. His birth was very different from the experience my husband and I shared during our first son's arrival. I was determined our second son would always feel as precious as our first—and never feel as if he was the "runner-up."

IT'S IMPORTANT FOR PARENTS TO UNDERSTAND IT'S OKAY THEIR SECOND CHILD HAS A VERY DIFFERENT EXPERIENCE IN COMING INTO THIS WORLD THAN THEIR FIRST DID—INCLUDING LESS FANFARE FROM OTHERS. Still, the second is EQUALLY special—in his or her own ways!!!!!!!!!!!!!!!!!!!!!!!!!

Number Two Should Fit like a Shoe!

A Pair of Shoes Is Better than One— The Second Boy Around.

When I became pregnant with my second child, I wanted, in so many ways, to make it as special as it was with my first. It took me a while to first recognize and then admit, although it could be just as special in its own way, it was impossible to be just like my first. Ultimately I discovered, like snowflakes, no two pregnancies are the same, but each is unique and beautiful in its own way.

From the beginning of my second pregnancy, everyone professed their happiness for my husband and I, especially since our first son, Derek, would be getting a sibling. Still, there seemed to be much less excitement, somewhat less hoopla surrounding his arrival.

Other's reactions were quite understandable given the fact I had given birth to Derek a mere 10 months earlier. Now, just as our first son was beginning to walk, I was announcing I was with child again.

Believe me, my husband and I—along with close friends and family—were in complete shock for a while from this surprise pregnancy. We were still trying to manage our lives with one child; the time went by too quickly for us to experience all the anticipation we were able to savor planning for our first birth.

When I finally processed the fact I was pregnant again, I thought, "Well, number two should fit like a shoe. Now we'll have a pair."

After all, I already went through an entire pregnancy: Some of my maternity clothes were still wearable; I knew about morning sickness from my first which, in my case, is a misnomer as it lasted for the entire day, throughout the entire pregnancy. Thankfully, half-way into my second pregnancy, I was able to eat a few more of the foods that had caused nausea a few months earlier.

I already knew my body—especially my stomach, which had hardly gotten back to its pre-pregnancy shape, would again stretch beyond what I thought was humanly possible. In fact, even my fingers and feet seemed to expand after my first pregnancy: I struggled forcing my wedding ring on, when it previously slid down my finger. My shoes now squeezed my toes similar to the way my "fat" jeans of yesteryear pinched my stomach.

With this second baby, I hoped to be more relaxed since I had mastered—to some degree—a few of the mothering skills so new to me before. I had invested much energy and love into breastfeeding my son for his first six months of life and consider it one of my greatest accomplishments. For reasons beyond my immediate awareness, I never imagined, before having my son—and before discussing it with my twin sister who breastfed—I would choose this option to nurture my baby.

Yet, once I researched the benefits and held our son in my arms, it was such a natural instinct to do so. I also knew if I breastfed my second, the diapers would be sweet smelling, that is, before I introduced solids. My husband appreciated my breastfeeding efforts even more when he had diaper changing duties.

Once we supplemented with formula in order to satisfy our son's ever increasing appetite, my husband gladly participated in the feedings. He too became skillful at this task—as well as swaddling, bathing, reading and playing with Derek—not to mention the wondrous stroller rides we both went on and the adventurous trips to various parks.

A major issue I faced with my first, and knew I would continue to struggle with after my second child, was managing time. A good rule to follow is: add at least an hour to getting ready for any planned activity or event, and if it's at your own home, add way more time than that. The best example I can share with any mom regarding underestimating the amount of time it will take getting yourself and the baby ready is going to your baby's monthly scheduled wellness appointments; I would race around my house, often unprepared for whatever mishap occurred. I struggled most with coordinating my baby's schedule with mine. At first I didn't consider factors such as his feeding, dressing and sleeping needs when I prepared. Other variables such as whether or not my son (or I) slept the night before, or what his (or my) mood was also contributed to how fast I was able to get out of the house. Thank goodness my husband was able to come with me for our first doctor's visit which was on a blustery winter morning. Getting the baby dressed and blanketed, along with readying his diaper bag, feeding and changing him and barely tending to myself sent me into a frenzy.

Now that I was having a second child, I had no illusion it would be an easy task bringing another baby on board! Ironically, I was notoriously known by those close to me for spending an inexcusable amount of time primping myself for outings prior to having my own child. It took giving birth for me to get in the "express" lane of self care. I'm sure my appearance reflected as such, but boy, did my son look polished!

Something I wasn't prepared for with our second was a quiet anticipation that seemed to surround us weeks prior to the birth date. With our first, our loved ones surprised us with a warm and wonderful baby shower and mini celebrations; we received many symbolic gifts representing magical baby moments including: Derek's first teddy bear; a silver fork and spoon; a ceramic plate and mug; a music box; a hand pieced quilt, a beginner train set, & even a few, homemade stuffed animals.

Plus, we were blessed to receive many practical gifts such as a crib, car seat, stroller, high chair, swing and more that would come in handy now—along with the many adorable outfits that Derek never even had a chance to wear or wore only once as he grew so quickly.

Coming from a large family, I often heard my younger sister complain about getting my hand-me-downs, so I began to worry our younger son might feel that way too. Then I realized how ridiculous I was being (it may have been my hormones) considering our second would be a baby for a while and wouldn't have any awareness of this—and when he did—he may not even care.

I learned from my first how quickly babies outgrow clothes and toys. As an admitted spendthrift, I loved buying clothes, books and toys for my son and so did my husband. He was especially enthusiastic about buying Derek's "boy stuff": his first baseball outfit, bat, glove, race track, and, of course, a football jersey. Unfortunately, we—along with grandparents, relatives and friends—overdid it!

For our second child, sensibility would play a bigger part in our family's purchasing choices as we faced financial struggles just buying lots more of the practical items that I now knew a newborn needed such as "onesies" and pajamas—not to mention the extra bibs and diapers that constantly need replenishing.

As my due date got closer, I gathered and surveyed the entire baby inventory we had saved from our first son's early months. We seemed to have all the necessities, and so I was comforted by that.

The anticipation I had with my first involved a lot about the newness of parenting and the life changes our family would go through. Now, my thought process was different: I wondered how I would love another child as deeply as my first. I questioned how Derek would adapt to the addition in our family. I contemplated what our first few months would be like. I hoped I would have enough energy to be a good mother to both of my children considering the sleep deprivation I experienced with Derek who was still waking throughout the night.

Intrinsically, I knew my second child would be different

than my first and I would be a different mother to him. I already was experiencing a dissimilar pregnancy in how I felt: My morning sickness wasn't as intense, I carried my second baby completely unlike my first, and, instead of the occasional swift kicking Derek loved to do, my second tickled me traveling in an intermittent up and down flurry—often leaving me giggling.

And, although I initially thought I was having a girl with my first pregnancy—and was obviously wrong—I knew this time, I was having a boy, despite most others who believed I would soon have a baby girl.

Yet, the most important metamorphosis I had undergone after my first pregnancy was learning to ultimately trust my "mother's instinct." I give Derek credit for teaching me to have confidence in my inner voice of wisdom and to listen to it.

Before I had my first son, my obstetrician, who I had complete faith in, transferred during the eighth month of my pregnancy, to a different, much less desirable, hospital —almost an hour away. Against my instincts, I agreed to let her male partner deliver Derek at our local hospital.

It's important to note that I had never really felt he was as competent as my first obstetrician, although he tried to act as if he was; In short, on a personal level, I never really liked him. Yet, I ignored the uneasiness I felt, which was later intensified when he made errors during Derek's delivery.

So, for my second pregnancy, I sought my original obstetrician—traveling the distance for her skill and understanding. She apologized for all the trouble we had with our first delivery, vowing to work with my husband and I. Given our history, she was extremely hesitant to convey difficult news to us about delivering our second child: I would most likely be her last delivery. As of June 30th of that year, she was leaving obstetrics to solely practice gynecology in order to have more time with her own family. Although I understood her wishes, I was frantic as my due date was July 3rd.

After the difficult situation we had with our first, my husband—who also underwent his own fatherhood transformation—agreed to support whatever choice I made. So, after weighing my options, I concluded I felt most comfortable having this obstetrician deliver our baby and agreed to be induced during the third week of June.

I put all the motions into play so my parents would care for our son, Derek, while I was in the hospital. I reviewed the procedure with the nurses who prepped me for what was to come; and I spoke with the doctor about what to expect.

However, once I got to the hospital, I felt uneasy: My voice within—"My Mother's Instinct"—told me I shouldn't force my son's birth simply because of a doctor's scheduling conflict. I questioned, "Why our son should be rushed from the safety of my womb in such an intrusive manner?"

The more I thought about it, the more upset I became—and the more confident I was in waiting for whatever was the "right" time for my son to be delivered. I shared my concerns and MY decision with my obstetrician, who apologized and agreed she didn't have the right to impose her needs above our child's. We left the hospital determined to let "Mother Nature" take her course while I, as this baby's mother, would take mine. I knew I had made the right choice for my baby and somehow everything was going to be okay!

That evening I talked to my baby calling him by the

name we had already chosen for him: Dylan Thomas. I asked him, if he was ready, to please join our family by the end of June. I continued to rub my belly several times every day and evening. I told my son how much we already loved him and how excited we were about his birth. I truly felt my son was listening and at ease, ready to partner with me on this journey of life. And he did!

I went into labor late during the evening of June 28th and delivered our second son on the 29th, one day to spare from our obstetrician's deadline.

During the delivery, instead of lying down flat as I had been instructed during my first birth, I stood in a squatting position, holding onto a bar as I pushed. My doctor never suggested I get an epidural as the previous obstetrician recommended. As the hours progressed and the labor intensified, my doctor advised me to go into the warm shower, located in the adjoining room. Within minutes, I dilated to ten centimeters, and intensely pushed several times before delivering my second, beautiful baby boy.

I knew from the moment I met Dylan he had touched my soul, as his brother had, and we had our own unique connection. I understood my love for him would grow stronger each day, and I would always make sure he felt as special as his brother.

I already sensed Dylan was a flexible, cooperative and agreeable boy and I would, in some way, show him how much I appreciated these qualities; It was almost as if Dylan knew that's what our family needed right now.

I also was confident—although Derek needed some time to make the adjustment—Dylan would be the best brother Derek could have hoped for, and we were blessed as a family to welcome this precious boy into our lives.

I thanked God for helping me trust my "Mother's Instinct" in planning for Dylan's birth—and I prayed to have enough wisdom to follow this guiding voice for the rest of our lives, as we grow stronger and closer as a family.

Reader Reflection

- What changes are you (have you, plan to) experiencing with your 2nd child?
- How is your second child similar/different than your first—and how are you different?

LESSON 4

"Play-dates for Playmates"
Whatever Happened to Making Mud Pies?

I went into a type of cultural shock when I became a stay-at-home mom with two boys. I wondered whatever happened to kids playing in neighborhoods and mothers having coffee "next door," as it was when my mom was raising us?

I discovered both mothers and their children often have to look farther for friends and set-up what's now called "play-dates" for children to spend time together.

I learned finding family "playmates" is similar to dating: It's challenging finding the right "match." I soon learned how to weed out a few of the "duds."

I'd like new moms to understand it may take a while before finding parents and children they can really have fun with. I wish someone had explained this process to me. It can be so much easier if a sister or a childhood friend has children the same age because an established bond already exists. With new moms and babies, ***everyone*** has to get to know each other during a time when each mom is adapting to her new motherhood role and all the changes that accompany it.

I realized some moms I met became acquaintances who I simply spent time with at school or at sport's events. In contrast, I developed lasting friendships with other women who I made a deeper connection with.

Remember it's not the quantity of the friends, but rather the quality of the time spent together, as well as the support you give to each other. It also may take several years to develop a meaningful bond with another parent.

"Play-dates for Playmates:"
Whatever Happened to Making Mud Pies?

Once our first son went to nursery school, I was excited he'd make some friends and I might find a few as well. Ironically, one of the moms who also had a son in Derek's class had been in my Lamaze group. Although I didn't remember her, I was so glad "Phyllis" recognized me during our preschool orientation visit, the day before the official start of school. Our sons were born only days apart, in the month of November, so we already had that connection.

She decided to have a small get together; something now called a "play-date," so some of the boys in the class could meet while the moms chatted. My husband agreed to watch our younger son, Dylan, so Derek could have some independent time to meet his new classmates.

I must admit, I took a little more time getting Derek (and myself) ready that morning as I wanted to make a good first impression. When we arrived, it was apparent all the other moms/children had also dressed to impress compared to the attire we had become accustomed to wearing for our trips to the park with toddlers in tow.

I couldn't believe the snacks and entrees Phyllis had prepared for us; she served several dishes and salads along with a variety of drinks that filled a huge cooler.

"So, this is what a 'play-date' is?" I wondered. It was a stark contrast to my own memories of early childhood play outside; I recalled a much different setting: Most of the time, my twin sister and I sat in front of our house on a huge green, enameled swing. As we rocked back and forth, often singing all our favorite songs, my twin and I had a front row seat to lots of action on the street. We'd watch our brothers and the neighborhood kids play baseball, tag and water balloon fights.

Periodically we'd get off the swing and join in. Other times we'd sit in our driveway, part concrete—part dirt, with empty coffee cans between our legs and spoons in our hands. A few friends from the block would join us as we filled the cans with dirt to make mud pies, castles, cities and fun places that we'd pretend to visit.

In comparison, my son was now playing in a beautifully manicured backyard filled with loads of toys and an awesome jungle gym. This was the setting most of our generation, including my husband and I, worked hard to provide for our children. It was interesting for me as I observed the children scurrying from one toy to the next, overwhelmed by so many choices. Ultimately, the children settled into one area to play with the trucks in the dirt while we moms got acquainted.

During our conversation, I admitted to Phyllis I wondered how she had gotten all this together while still taking care of her two small boys. I confessed, and the other moms concurred, with the lack of sleep I was getting, along with the constant care my two sons—both under the age of three—required, I would not attempt such an ambitious task. We joked that Phyllis was "making us look bad."

Phyllis was a hard act to follow, so I opted for a simpler "play-date" and invited Phyllis and her two boys over. Still, I struggled as I sorted the toys and organized the house the night before. Once I got the kids bathed and in bed, I decided I should cook something special for Phyllis as she had gone to so much trouble in preparing food for us. So, in addition to the regular sandwiches and munchies I made for the kids, I decided to cook vegetable lasagna for Phyllis who is a vegetarian. I didn't realize it would take so long to prepare. I didn't start until 9pm and was cooking past midnight. When I went to sleep that morning, I remember hoping the day went well including the kids and adults getting along.

When they came to our house, we played at the park across the street from us before coming to our home. They stayed for a few hours as we had lunch before exploring my sons' toys. Happily we all connected and had a great "date."

As time went on, a group of us moms had each other over on a rotating basis. Although it was a great experience, in many ways, for both the children and the adults, it was—at times—overwhelming. Sometimes a child or parent would feel left out of the group, or the children would argue over a toy or tantrum when they had to leave.

Plus, I would spend so much time cleaning and preparing for visits only to have a mess when everyone left; I know the same was probably true for the other moms.

Yet, I found only a few who confessed to how much work it was. I truly believe some women thrive under pressure and can handle it with ease. Other women, like me, felt pressured to live-up to a certain standard as part of being a "good" mother.

I fooled some people I too was a "supermom." I even remember one mother who I befriended calling after finding a "Baby Gap" jacket at her house. "I thought it was yours," she inquired, adding, "but once I saw a stain on the jacket, I knew it wasn't as your children are always so immaculately dressed."

I had mixed emotions about her perception. Initially, I was flattered she—and maybe others—thought I took great pride in dressing my children. But I knew the view that my rugged little boys are always pristinely dressed is as much false as it is ridiculous. I mean, seriously, my kids are always playing outside in the dirt; many of the stains on their clothes still remain as I have been unable to remove them, even through several washings.

My friend's comment made me wonder if I was trying too hard to present the appearance of perfection by dressing my children in their "better" clothes and cleaning my house hours before their visits. It took me time to find a balance of allowing friends over even when my house wasn't immaculate and letting my kids wear their clean but stained clothes when we went out.

I was so surprised when a new mom we met at preschool invited me, along with several other moms, to her home that was in complete disarray. Some of the other women thought it was a disgrace she didn't clean-up before our visit. I too was astonished by the "mess," but more inspired by her nonchalant attitude: I truly respected her for not caring so much about appearances. She was more interested in the children having fun and in the engaging conversation we shared along with our coffee.

Although I still would be uncomfortable inviting guests into an unkempt house, once I became better acquainted with some moms, I was more forgiving of my own housekeeping imperfections. I realized children and their parents need to be free to play, make messes and enjoy life—to a certain degree. I also found it absolutely therapeutic to have "play-dates" with moms, who like me, were thrilled to meet at a park—which is a neutral ground where no one has to worry about damaging anyone's homes or belongings contained therein.

I tried to carry this perspective when it came to birthday celebrations as well—especially after my father confided he thought my son's birthday party was more like a wedding. Ironically, compared to the elaborate indoor playground parties, pony rides and rented castles, our "construction worker" party, held at our home when Derek was four, seemed tame in comparison.

Yet, there have been times I admit to going overboard when it comes to my children's parties. I believe some parents, including us, have these elaborate events, in part, more for ourselves than the young toddlers.

It may be an opportunity to entertain, socialize and connect with women as there are little opportunities for moms to do this while caretaking. Even during the rare occasions when we do get together, much of the time we are discussing our children or following them around due to safety concerns.

When I was a little girl it seemed that moms had more support from each other: We lived on a street where most of the mothers borrowed sugar from the house next door. Parents would come outside to chat in the early evenings and for social gatherings. In short, most of the moms felt like they were "in the same boat," a house boat that floated in a neighborhood where they knew each other and their children played outside on the sidewalks and in the street.

Our grandparents lived only a few blocks away from our home and we saw them weekly. Our relatives, for the most part, lived nearby so they would visit us for holidays and get-togethers throughout the year.

Today, in contrast, developments have, in many instances, replaced neighborhoods. In fact, many people don't even know who their neighbors are. Families are often separated by several states, so working couples may hire caretakers, frequently from other countries, to help with their children.

When I had my first child soon after moving into a new development, I felt isolated and somewhat estranged from the world. There wasn't any family close by. I did meet some neighbors who were nice. Most of them had older children and wanted to sit and have coffee. I was seeking women who also had young toddlers who my children could have opportunities to play with while we moms had time to get to know each other.

As time went on, I realized it can be a lonely day, especially after experiencing several sleepless nights. Some mornings I barely had enough energy to shower. Like other moms, who constantly care for their family, I often neglected myself. I realized it was vital for me to forge new relationships with other moms who do understand these trials and tribulations—and who too are seeking balance in their lives. In addition to the moms I met from my children's activities, I took a few adult-ed classes and attended parent/toddler groups for support.

I also invested energy in maintaining the few genuine friendships I had established with the people who have accepted, encouraged and nurtured the changes and growth in my life. These family and friends have become my salvation.

I discovered I can only be a great mom if I am a happy person. Having a social network, even a small one, enables me to reach out to other women who I can enjoy life's celebrations with, confide my secrets to and seek/provide support for each other's challenges.

P.S. Recently a few of the moms who accompanied me to the 'messy" house for a "play-date," shared some news: This mom has now hired a housekeeper because she joined a kickboxing class. Now, I'm confident those judgmental moms won't "mess" with her again!

Reader Reflection

- What experiences have you had in finding "play-dates" for you and your child(ren)?
- Share fun times, horror stories, amazing insights???

LESSON 5

Identical Twins:
There's More than Meets the Eye When Raising Twins and Other Siblings—Especially When Twins/Siblings Become Moms.

After traveling through some rocky terrain, my twin and I discovered the only expectations we must fulfill are the ones we set for ourselves. My twin and I now share a sisterhood connection that has grown even stronger since we both have our own children.

It's because of this unique birthright I hoped my son would receive the gift of a brother. And he did! Although they still are young, my boys already have an amazing friendship, even if they don't always appreciate it—like during long car rides when they both want to play with the same toy. In time I know they will nurture and treasure the brotherly bond they have formed even more as we try to recognize each of their unique personas.

The closeness my twin and I share is mirrored by

the relationship our children have with their cousins; my boys and my sister's girls became ONE family from the moment they met!

So, whether you have one child or several, it's important to foster family bonding while instilling confidence by highlighting each child's individuality. This strengthens all family members' self-esteem while also encouraging harmonious sibling relationships—as well as those with cousins and friends!!!!!!!!!!!!!!!!!!!!!!!

Identical Twins:
There's More than Meets the Eye When Raising Twins and Other Siblings—Especially When Twins/Siblings Become Moms

As a new mother of two boys—only 18 months apart in age—I was given lots of advice on how to raise them properly, especially tips to guard against sibling rivalry. Many onlookers mistook my boys for twins, which often caused me to share some of my own childhood experiences growing up as an identical twin along with some lessons I learned.

Almost everyone thought I was someone else. I could understand strangers, relatives and even friends confusing the two of us. But when my own mother mistook me for my identical twin sister and smacked my bottom for decorating the kitchen with cornflakes, I knew, as young as I was, it would be a struggle to be an "I" instead of a "we" for the rest of my life.

Can you imagine how disappointing it was as a toddler to race to the Christmas tree only to find that my "other half" had already opened her presents?; mine were usually duplicates.

Or how about the sadness I felt when my boyfriend of three years confused the two of us on prom night? I remember the pleasantly amused expressions on my parent's faces as he approached my twin with MY corsage. Those amused smiles quickly changed to sympathizing frowns when they saw my tormented eyes. Did someone exist who was exactly like me?

For our entire childhood, people have constantly confused and compared me with my twin sister. "Are you Donna or Debbie?" is a question I'll probably be asked for the rest of my life. "Which one is older?" has been a controversial inquiry since my mother is confident I was born first, even though our birth certificates state my sister is four minutes older than I am.

"How do you tell them apart?" has been the most dreaded of all queries as it triggers an examination process whereby baffled onlookers study and search every inch of our beings for clues to our mistaken identities. A day seldom passed without someone commenting on which one of us was "prettier," "smarter" or "nicer."

Because we received this constant attention, my sister and I knew we were different from our peers. Still, we were not prepared for the social and emotional encounters twins are often forced to deal with. In fact, it has taken my sister and I many years to learn and convey one message: Even though we look alike, we are two separate and wonderful people, each with her own persona.

Our relationship was intensified when our family moved from the city to the suburbs during our adolescence, a challenging time in and of itself. Naturally, we missed the shared friends we had made and the environment we had grown so accustomed to. The suburbs seemed like a desolate countryside.

Our father thought it would be "cute" if Debbie and I wore the same outfits for our first day of school: crisp, white-ruffled blouses tucked inside ankle-length pleated, plaid skirts of orange and brown. It was a stark contrast to the leisurely attire of T-shirts and jeans worn by most of the other students.

We received instant attention as we walked down the long corridors, lined with clusters of surveying eyes. Debbie had the same look of relief when the bell rang and the students disappeared into their classrooms. When we walked into the class, another barrage of eyes was on us—as whispering spread across the room.

"Hey, here comes the Bobsey Twins," yelled a snide freckled-faced boy. "You two don't need mirrors," he snickered.

Word of our arrival was publicized quickly. As if we were commodities, students and teachers alike came to get a share of the "identical twins." Debbie and I were bombarded by questions, wisecracks and analysis. It was as if we were being dissected.

In time, like anyone or anything that is "different," we were accepted. The comparisons, however, continued. In school, our appearances and personalities were constantly compared; at home our report cards were viewed side by side. My twin and I were being forced deeper and deeper into a rivalry. Back then, we didn't realize we should have been on the same battlefield.

As tension began to build in our relationship, we sought

means of differentiating ourselves. We desperately wanted others to accept us as twins, and also recognize our distinct attributes. The first outward statement of our individuality was in our appearance. Even though we owned the same outfits, we wore them on alternating days and swapped the different clothing we owned.

Next, we chose opposite companions and interests. We barely spoke to each other, unless we fought, sometimes physically. It was as if each of us was trying to destroy that part of her the other had come to possess. Discontented at our belligerent behavior, my father repeatedly echoed, "One day you'll realize how lucky you are to be twins. Instead of fighting, you should be helping each other."

Well, one day came soon enough. As I was sitting in the school cafeteria, I saw one of my new "friends" giggling as my twin walked by. I later found out she was making fun of my sister's brightly colored blouse. I was fuming mad—as red as the crimson from Debbie's shirt—and yelled at my no longer "friend." I realized my sister was more important to me than any of the girls in my grade. I was ashamed I had been so impressed with supposed "cool" girls, and that I had treated my twin so poorly. I made a decision to put my sister—my twin—first.

My sister and I worked on becoming reacquainted and strengthening bonds with friends who accepted us both as individuals and as twins. Debbie and I also learned of two upperclassmen who wanted to date us.

Once we dated, my sister and I realized we were attracted to each other's boyfriends. Now, on common ground again, we did something we were used to doing our entire life: we swapped! Although we eventually broke-up with our boyfriends, our sisterhood continued to flourish, even when we went to separate colleges.

Debbie and I would talk for hours on the phone each week. No one seemed to understand me as she did. After all, we had gone from diapers through dating together. And when she did visit me at school, my friends were amazed not only by our physical similarities, but also by our common mannerisms and philosophies. My closest college friend said, "I knew what your sister's response would be before she responded; it was exactly like yours."

After I graduated from college, I had a romantic break-up that left me heartbroken. Not knowing what to do, I instinctively picked-up the phone and called my twin who, due to a career opportunity, lived in another state.

"Donna, are you okay?" she answered. "I've been worried about you all day." I perfunctorily shared the news of my break-up, desperately pretending I was okay.

When I heard silence, I indignantly replied, "Don't you have any response?" I heard a quiet weeping from my sister, "I know how important he was to you, and I can *feel* the pain that you are feeling." When I hung-up the phone, I thanked God that someone was so much like me—MY TWIN!

Although my sister and I pursued different aspirations after graduating college, we remained best friends. Our lives took separate directions as I fervently pursued my advertising ambitions, while Debbie headed to the altar.

As her Maid of Honor, I invited her for a rendezvous Caribbean Cruise which I was awarded for my professional accomplishments. Us city-born girls snorkeled by day and partied at night, loving all the pampering and attention we received.

When we returned and celebrated her amazing wedding, I was saddened she now lived 5-driving hours away. In the year that followed, Deborah (which is the name she now wanted to be called) became pregnant and asked me to be Godmother to her first-born.

When she finally went into labor, I felt helpless several states away despite her bringing an 8" x 10" photo of me into the delivery room to use as her "focal" point. That night I waited to hear news. I fell asleep at 1:00am and woke at exactly 6:15am that morning declaring Deborah had a baby girl—not a boy—as everyone had predicted. Several hours later, my brother-in-law called announcing Deborah gave birth to "Christina," at 6:15a.m. Amazingly, I had awakened at the *precise* moment "Christina" came into this world.

Some years later when I married my husband and eventually had two sons, Deborah cheered us on. Although I joined some parent/infant groups, I sought my twin for much advice, especially since so many onlookers had forecasted much sibling rivalry between my two children "so close in age." My husband comforted me often saying he and his brother, who have a seven year age difference, had many competitive and challenging times during their upbringing. I decided my boys would learn to work through their differences while still developing their individuality.

Upon meeting other moms at the playground or related events, they often ask me lots of questions about raising my boys. Once they discover I have an identical twin sister, lots of inquiries follow, especially if they have or knew of someone with twins or other multiples—including children close in age. I oblige with answers, often highlighting the wonderful fun we had buying our clothes together as youngsters, the synergistic connection we had exemplified in situations such as when we both earned the exact SAT scores in high school, to our mischievous antics of swapping boyfriends…to the even deeper connection we now have as mothers. Our journey has led us to ultimately cherish the unique birthright we are privy to.

I think it's equally important to explain some of our struggles growing-up and how we learned to deal with them in order to embrace our twinhood. In fact, it has taken my sister and I years to learn and convey one message: although we are a fabulous duo, we each are amazing individuals who must only fulfill the expectations we employ for ourselves. I have become my sister's number one fan encouraging her acting and singing pursuits while she supports my many writing endeavors!!

I know—being the twin I am—I should think TWICE before giving any parenting advice, but, I believe, parents—including those of twins—would benefit by gathering as much information and guidance about the challenges most twins and siblings are confronted by. And who better to share this unique insight than a TWIN HERSELF!

First and most importantly, each twin—like every child—needs to feel she is a special individual. So many times my sister and I were referred to as "the twins," by well meaning people in our lives, instead of by our separate names. After a while, we began to feel like one entity, as if we were a pair of shoes, barely distinguishable except one of us was the left and the other, the right. So, we gently reminded everyone what our names were and responded once we were called by them. It's so important to remember, even if each twin looks similar and has shared interests, recognize and nurture each twin's persona—her strengths, aspirations and talents.

The key to mastering this philosophy is to keep all doors of communication open. As with all siblings, parents should schedule alone or "special" time for doing an activity of each sibling's choice—even if it's just to have a conversation. By doing this with each sibling, a bond is fostered. Then when situations arise that children have trouble handling, they're more likely to feel comfortable discussing them with adults.

Additionally, it's critical for parents to validate their children's feelings, even if they don't understand them. Having family discussions with all children is a key ingredient found in many successful families.

Dressing alike is a topic so many parents of twins wonder about; in fact, the ones whom I've met have always asked me about this subject. I love dressing my boys in the same or similar outfits; yet, once they're old enough, I will invite them to share their thoughts about clothing choices—and I advise other parents of twins and siblings to let their children decide as well. Preferences may change during different times during their lives. They may even want to dress alike at times and differently for other occasions. And this can change as they grow.

For example, I know my twin and I loved dressing alike as toddlers all the way through sixth grade. Then, when our family moved from the Bronx to the suburbs, we changed our minds. Starting at a new school had been difficult enough without being viewed under a microscope: Students and teachers alike had been comparing us so much that we were compelled to express our individuality through our attire.

By discussing the issues facing each set of twins—and other children in the family—adults can prepare all siblings for situations they may encounter—and model possible responses. I know for my sister and I this would have been extremely helpful in dealing with all the insensitive comparisons made and ridiculous questions onlookers often asked.

Additionally, our younger sister, who always felt "left out" because no one ever made a "big deal" about her, would have also benefited from these discussions. My twin and I often explain to her how much we disliked the constant attention we received—however positive it may have been intended—because it often prompted judgmental comments.

Until we learned how to respond, most of the time we remained silent, often feeling badly for the twin who was relegated to "second place."

As we grew, we learned appropriate responses to these unfair critiques. We began using light sarcasm and laughter as powerful tools. When asked which of us is prettier, for example, I might say, "Oh, my sister, of course. She's gorgeous and I look just like her."

Or, to the question: "Which one of you is nicer," I have responded. "Neither of us; we're both double trouble." A big grin usually seals the response nicely.

Equally important is for each set of twins or siblings to be treated as a one of a kind "partnership." This is important because people often make generalizations about twins or sibling relationships because they know other families with twins/children and think there are steadfast rules that govern all.

Decisions about children, including twins, are specific

to every family's situation. This is why when parents of twins ask me questions such as whether or not their twins should be placed in the same class or wear some kind of outward statement, such as a ring or pierced earrings, to differentiate one twin from another, the best answer I can give them is, "it's a personal choice," based on the circumstances unique to each household.

I also assure parents if they make mistakes, as all parents do, they can make adjustments and move forward. For example, twins in one of my children's classes were separated during nursery school at the Director's recommendation. Once in Kindergarten, the parents, based on feedback from the twins, made a request for their twins to be placed in the same class.

With my own children, I discovered each flourished in completely different environments during nursery school: one son benefited with more structure while my younger one enjoyed more creative play. Hence, much in the same way twins should be celebrated as individuals, so should *all siblings*.

Sometimes parents get additional encouragement just talking to other parents or finding general support groups. Others may benefit from more specific groups as those that focus, for example, on topics for parents of multiples. By selectively implementing the useful information/strategies gained from positive parent resources, children will feel treasured for their uniqueness and transfer those special feelings to their own children and generations to come.

Even though my twin sister lives in a different state, I share an indescribable bond with her. When our children—her three girls and my two boys—are together, it's as if we are **one family**—and it was like this from the moment our children met. As adults, we still have similar styles in clothing and food preferences; we often buy each other identical items and spend holidays and summer vacations together!

Now when we're out, we relish onlooker's attention and hope one day to do commercials and/or pursue other twin-related endeavors; we may use the same pitch we used when we launched our babysitting career at age 12: "two for the price of one."

Reader Reflection

- How have your relationships with your siblings impacted mothering your child(ren)?
- What important sibling lessons do you want to pass on to your child(ren)?

LESSON 6

My Friend, "Aunt Margi" —
"Wild and Crazy" to "Thursday Night Shoppers"

Lifelong friends allow us to cross the bridge of time from past to present—always looking forward to tomorrow together. My best friend Margi is a lifeline for me; no matter how old we become, we're still comfortable acting like silly teenagers experiencing life to the fullest. She's been there for me through good and bad times, experiencing my joys and sorrows.

Margi's love and friendship extended unconditionally to my children and that makes her even more special! One of my greatest hopes is that each of my sons finds a true friend, one who will enhance the closeness they share as brothers and who will relish exploring the wondrous world with them!

It's vital for women to nurture those close childhood friendship(s), if given the opportunity; If they do, they'll have someone in their life who

has a shared history with them—someone who knows them—first as a child, then as a woman, before ever knowing them as a MOM!!!!!!!!!!!!!!

My Friend, "Aunt Margi"—
"Wild and Crazy" to "Thursday Night Shoppers."

My best friend, Margi and I have developed a strong familial bond. Both my twin and I think of her as a sister.

When we first met Margi, we had no idea of the impact she would have on our lives, nor did we understand what we perceived as ordinary childhood experiences would, over time, transform into extraordinary, lifelong memories we could build upon as our friendship evolved.

During sixth grade, my twin sister and I met Margi after moving from the Bronx to the suburbs. Soon after we settled into our new suburban home, a girl we had met while visiting our cousin's, several blocks away, came by bicycle to welcome us to the town. Along her route, she met Margi cycling and invited her to bike along to meet us, the "new twins" in the neighborhood. Margi, always up for an adventure, agreed.

From the moment we met, Margi made us laugh demonstrating wild bicycle moves; we could tell she was a friendly and easy going free-spirit.

In school, my sister Deborah and I were placed on different teams; I was lucky enough to have Margi on mine. Even though I was overwhelmed by all the changes, in time, Margi and I were giggling and getting into what I call "inconspicuous" mischief.

Some of the other girls wanted to sit with me during class, but Margi became possessive. They began to argue about who and where my desk would be placed. I loved all the attention and felt welcome! My twin and I developed separate friendships, except for a few friends who we shared—especially Margi. In time, I began to spend every weekend with Margi hanging out at the park, mall—even the local bowling alley.

What once was a boring Friday night began to get "interesting" as adventures were born—hysterically bizarre scenarios seemed to follow us wherever we went.

During one of our shopping trips to the mall, we got stuck in the elevator located in a major department store. We were with some other friends, one of whom was hyperventilating. Another girl said she didn't think we were going to "make it out alive." It was very dramatic. Margi, my twin and I were cracking jokes, including making some "inappropriate comments," which we later found out were echoed by way of the speaker system throughout the store. When the elevator doors finally opened, we were greeted by an audience of laughter and applause.

One evening after leaving a party a little before midnight, Margi and I walked home. Both of us have been bitten by dogs and are terrified of them. So, naturally whenever we are together, we seem to somehow meet up with them.

We were only a few blocks away from my home when this black mutt darted from his yard and accosted us.

We stood frozen while the dog intimidated us with his seething growls and ferocious barking. Margi and I hugged each other and remained still for what seemed like hours. When we tried to slowly inch our way down the road, the dog became agitated and began his intimidation again—this time nipping at the bottom seams of our pants, sometimes snapping at our ankles. We started screaming—especially loud was Margi.

"Help," we called out.

Although we were petrified, we each began to find the humor in literally being held hostage by this two-foot high, fanged menace. We started bargaining with the dog for our freedom, promising to bring him back some sirloin tips. We even offered him a date with a female dog who lived nearby.

When that didn't work, I laughingly promised a bite from Margi's leg as I tried to separate from her. This time she screamed even louder. Thankfully, the owner of the home lifted his bedroom window and whistled for "Precious" (he certainly was not precious to us) to return to his yard. "Precious" dutifully obeyed his owner and retreated. We couldn't believe the owner simply slammed the window shut without saying a word, not even an apology.

We walked away from the "crime scene" threatening, under our breaths, of course, to sue for "mental and physical cruelty," maybe "kidnapping"—or we laughed—"dog-napping?'"

Our friendship grew throughout that first summer as a group of us went for a vacation with Margi's family to the Jersey Shore where we were beaching by day and partying at night. Cash poor, we actually devised a plan where only one of us would have to pay to get all of us onto the beach. Whoever paid first received a pin and piece of material to attach to her bathing suit as proof of payment by the beach personnel. Once the "payee" was on the beach, she'd detach the material and pin it onto a Frisbee—before flinging it over the boardwalk fence to where we waited.

Once the Frisbee was sent over, one of us would take the material from the Frisbee and pin it to her bathing suit before walking past the attendee and onto the beach. We would continue this process until all of us were on the beach. After devising this plan and other schemes to have summer fun—despite a lack of funds—we adopted the phrase, "Where's There's a Will, There's a Way!"

When we came back and school started, there was lots of hype among our classmates promoting and equating "coolness" with smoking. I succumbed to the peer pressure and tried it. I learned how to inhale and spent much of the summer teaching Margi: We'd race to our secret hiding place across the street from my home, quickly running barefoot down my neighbor's hill into a creek. Once in the creek, we'd hop from rock to rock, chasing the water as it meandered downstream until we reached an underground tunnel where we'd sit and puff away. After hours of shared conversation or happily sitting in complete silence—soothed by the sounds of the trickling water—we'd cavort home leaving ringlets of smoke dancing behind.

Unfortunately, Margi was caught smoking at school as well as getting into some other mischief; this prompted Margi's mother to take her out of public school and place her in an all girl Catholic Academy—until she "straightened out."

It was difficult when she left our school, but we still saw each other on weekends, often at the roller rink where we pretended to be much older when high school boys asked us to skate. I even had my first sleep over at her house after an early evening of skating, followed by a scary movie we saw at the local theatre. By the time we got home, we weren't tired so we stayed up till early morning giggling about boys and sharing secrets.

We laughed as Margi told stories about the strict nuns and how the girls at school practically attacked the custodians since there were no boys around. The upside of her new school was Margi was getting into less trouble while her grades were going up.

Although I missed her terribly, the older boy I had a crush on for over a year had become my boyfriend—and later—the first love of my life. He was several years older and outwardly quite confident as the quarterback for the school football team. We had a lot of fun, although it was at the expense of diminished time with own friends, especially Margi and my twin sister.

After my boyfriend graduated, I still had several years of high school to finish. I was elated when Margi's Mom agreed she could come back to public school during our junior year!

By now, my twin and I—plus a few other friends—were ready to have another pal to share our final two high school years with; we laughed so much that one of the teachers often jokingly asked us is we were drinking alcohol while several classmates nicknamed us, "Four, Wild and Crazy American Girls."

As tradition had it, we went to Washington, D.C. for our

senior trip. Our bus driver, "Earl" was a wild and crazy guy himself. In response to our screams to drive faster, he began racing with some of the other highway drivers. A police officer pulled him over, and gave him a ticket. This elevated "Earl" to the status of "cool," although, our parents didn't feel the same way when they heard about the incident.

Besides doing the Alley Cat dance and the Hokey Pokey on the bus, we also played a game called, "how many people can we fit in the bathroom on the bus;" the answer, we discovered, is 11 high school students. We encountered more difficulty trying to dislodge ourselves from the tiny space.

In Washington we had a fun time touring the Smithsonian trying to absorb all the history while we also jokingly posed with some of the famous statues.

At night we went dancing with the other students and teachers. Uninhibited, Margi was showcasing her moves on top of the tables and throughout the room. Margi does things I might think about doing, but am too self conscious to actually do in public—although there have been times when I've been inspired to let my wild side out.

The return bus trip was quieter and more reflective. As I stared out the window, images, like our lives, were passing before me. I realized it didn't matter what we did or where we were, as long as the four of us were together experiencing these magical moments.

The black and white class photo each of us has as a keepsake is a vivid reminder, memorializing our fun in Washington. Each of us—cool and collectively—appear twice in the photo. As the panoramic camera scanned across the class, we first were photographed in the upper left row with students, before sprinting as the camera moved, to again pose—cool and sassy—in the upper right.

Once we finished our senior year, it was time for us four friends to go to college and explore the world. I was excited and nervous, but I knew I wanted to go to college. My boyfriend, who by now I had discovered was inwardly insecure, wanted me to marry him. Luckily, I knew then I would resent him in the future if I didn't pursue my education and discover the woman I was destined to become! After many tears, I ultimately realized, as my Nana would say, "we weren't meant to be."

Thankfully, I was busy with college life and working to make money to help pay for it. Margi went away to college and during breaks we would visit each other. We got summer jobs together as waitresses in a Texas-styled rib and chicken restaurant. The boss and male cooks were eccentric and extremely picky as they yelled and even cursed at us. We laughed through a lot of ridiculousness to support each other. Once, for example, the boss went on a rant because I had two stirrers in a drinking glass instead of one. Another time he punished Margi and I for being late by taking us off the schedule for an entire week, which just gave us more time to get into more mischief!

After college, Margi became a travel agent and helped me realize a childhood dream: Going to Europe! It took me years of saving and getting up enough nerve before actually booking the trip.

While I was in Italy, I called Margi on her birthday; at first, she seemed depressed because her boyfriend didn't make a big deal about her special day. As always, I was able to cheer her up!

However, I didn't know it would be the most expensive

call I ever made. I still remember the concierge eyes widen when he looked at the bill—which seemed low to me—that is, until I realized the dollar amount was totaled in lira. It was almost $300. American dollars!

Margi and I get sentimental when we reminisce about that conversation—continents apart; it reminds us of those MasterCard commercials in which the commentator lists the high cost of items related to an event before highlighting the ultimate importance of spending "priceless" moments together.

I think all the moments we have spent together, the good and the challenging, are our foundation, the history we have created for us to reflect and rely upon. It helps us celebrate milestones—as well as deal with some of the heartache in our lives:

While I was coming home by plane from a vacation in Arizona, I suddenly felt something was terribly wrong with Margi. I used the plane phone to call her and sadly learned her Mom had died that morning.

Soon after this loss, Margi moved away to pursue her career. Neither one of us knew what turns our lives would take when we said our goodbyes.

We did know no matter what the distance, we'd always be friends—and one day we would again create more mischief, magic and memorable moments together!

In the years that followed, I had visits with Margi, but I missed her living close by—especially since my now married twin sister lived several hours away. I realized how special Deborah and Margi had been in my life and how we were always there for each other beginning in adolescence, an awkward time when most of us are struggling to "fit-in" and truly need someone to talk to about all the life decisions and transitions taking place.

When major changes were again going on in my life, I wished for their closeness. I had met other friends and acquaintances; still, no one knew me as Margi and my twin sister did—and neither of them lived near.

I was absolutely ecstatic when Margi advised me she accepted a job offer in the same state where I live, just in time to be my Maid of Honor—and to later share in the birth of our children.

As soon as Margi learned our first son, Derek, had a rough journey into this world, she rushed to a church before coming to see us at the hospital. Margi told us she was so upset to find the church locked; she began to frantically bang on the doors hoping for someone to open them. When no one came, she knelt on the outside stairs and prayed, begging God to protect our son. It touched my heart to hear this!

Once she held Derek, Margi proclaimed, and we agreed, he was the most beautiful boy she had ever seen. It's important to note most of my relatives and friends, for whatever reasons, favor baby girls and love to dote on them. Margi is the only friend I have who absolutely prefers and adores boys, which makes her an even better friend to me!!

In time, Derek healed and was able to come home—intensely loved from the moment of birth by our family and by my best friend who had a birth of her own: She became "Aunt Margi."

It was amazing to me my son had an instant connection with Margi, so much so that, besides his grandparents and my twin sister, she is the only one who is as intensely interested and sincerely proud of my son's accomplishments. She lets me rattle and prattle on about everything from Derek's voracious appetite to all his milestones of crawling, walking and soon after—sprinting at ten months old—the perfect time for an unexpected gift; I was pregnant again!

More than half-way into my second pregnancy, Margi and I had a disagreement and hadn't been talking for several weeks. I received a phone call from her fiancé explaining Margi had been in a terrible car crash and was in the hospital. I was huge, only a few days away from my delivery due-date, so it was difficult moving around.

Still, with my 18-month son in tow, I rushed to the hospital and waddled through the corridors to her room. The instant she saw me, she burst into tears, crying "I can't believe you came." I joked she didn't have to do something so drastic to get me to visit—we could have mended our differences over the phone; we both laughed as we hugged.

It turned out a wayward truck had crossed the double line into her lane of traffic head on during a rain storm. Margi was badly bruised and had major leg damage that took several surgeries and two years of physical therapy to only partially mend. There still are times when her leg pains her.

She really was, according to the doctors, "lucky to be alive." Ironically, the day of her accident was the same date of her mother's death, ten years earlier. So, we both know "Mom" was watching over her.

At the hospital, Margi and I realized how silly our argument had been compared to the depth of our friendship; we declared we would make it a priority to spend time together, especially as our lives would be taking such different directions: I was having a another baby which would make Margi a doting and loving aunt for the second time.

In complete contrast with my so called "life plan," I chose to be a "stay at home mom." after my second son, Dylan Thomas, was born. Margi's life was going in another direction as she was promoted to a higher level corporate travel position.

Since my husband was often able to get home earlier on Thursday evenings, Margi and I agreed we would schedule "girls' night out." As we both love to shop, we began visiting our local mall as we did when we were kids. It's from these frequent visits that we have befriended several mall employees who nicknamed us, "The Thursday Night Shoppers."

Even if we don't buy anything, we sit at the food court, chatting away. Sometimes we sip coffee and eat chocolate—or get dinner and ice-cream as we did when we were teenagers getting into mischief.

My husband and children encourage my dates with Margi because they recognize I'm happier after my Thursday night out.

It gives me an opportunity to truly be myself with someone who I trust completely! I can talk with her about anything which is such a welcome reprieve from solely spending time with other moms. I still discuss my children with Margi as they have become my life, but I can do so with someone who brags more about my boys than I do!

Plus, Margi provides me with a connection to the outside world so I can live vicariously through her career experiences, including the worldly travel she pursues—not to mention listening to the juicy office "gossip."

Margi jokes that she doesn't have any of her own children

because she has "trouble" taking care of herself, but my family and I agree she'd be an amazing mom. She recently rescued a dog from the pound who she named Amy and who she worships like her own child.

My kids love their Aunt Margi who they recognize is all about having fun. She adores coming to their birthday parties and for Christmas/New Year celebrations. She's even planned several "back to school" parties for my boys.

When my kids are off from school, we occasionally visit Margi at her office for lunch. The cafeteria, as my children say, is "awesome" with all different food stations. Best of all there is a huge dessert section and cappuccino niche. There's even a company store to buy lots of goodies. When we visit her, everyone calls my kids "Margi's nephews" and we get the VIP treatment—taking home lots of store items and little favors to remember our day.

I recently gave Margi a surprise "40th" birthday party at my home. My children loved secretly planning the event with ideas for the food selection, guests and presents.

Margi was visibly moved and truly shocked when she arrived. It was a wonderful time as we talked about all the magical times we had. Others at the party listened and laughed at our amusing stories from the past.

For Margi and I—it was as if we were actually experiencing these moments again—back in time together. We have grown to have our individual lives while still sharing a common perspective, a history. It's this visceral connection of often knowing what the other is thinking or feeling that is the tree trunk of our friendship, one that we lean on when we encounter some of life's triumphs as well as its struggles.

It's why till this day, if we're sitting in the same room,

Margi and I marvel at how we can laugh at an incident or situation that others may not find any humor in.

Since the birth of my children, many new people have come in and out of our family's lives. Sometimes there are outside circumstances, shared interests or a convenience the friendship develops from—such as spending time with parents whose children play on our children's soccer team or meeting another mom at an adult exercise class.

When the season or class ends, the friendship may continue. In some instances, the relationship doesn't develop into anything more than a mere acquaintance. These experiences helped my husband and I realize who our dearest friends are: the few, like Margi, who have always been "there" for us whether in person or in spirit during the celebrations and through the rough waters—supporting our family's journey and us supporting theirs.

Often when Margi and I are out together, we see other teenage girls whispering their secrets and giggling. I know exactly how they feel! I wonder if their friendships will grow stronger in the years to come.

If they're as lucky as I am, they'll always feel childlike and special when they're together, as I do with Margi.

So, if you see two forty-something, spunky women giggling and acting like their shoe size—rather than their age—know that it's us: "Aunt Margi" and Me!

Reader Reflection

- Who is your best friend and why?
- How has she supported your transformation into motherhood and how has your relationship evolved?

LESSON 7

Some Wonderful Things Can Happen if the North Meets the South—
My Boys, My Joys: A Tale of Opposites!

My Nana always said, "Opposites Attract," but I never thought about this premise until I was an adult. I discovered I am attracted to people who are different from me—including my husband who looks and acts contrary to the way I do. It's no wonder we have children who are "night" and "day"—often referred to as the "odd couple."

We learned each family member balances another so everyone finds his niche, and like a magnificent quilt, once all the pieces come together, an exquisite work of art is formed—our family!!

Other families I've spoken with, whether they've included boys, girls or both, agree their children

are completely opposite from each other. So, get prepared to learn, just when you think you understand one child, another child will confuse and surprise you beyond belief!!!!!!!!!!!!

Some Wonderful Things Can Happen if the North Meets the South
My Boys, My Joys: A Tale of Opposites!

I feel like the rope in a game of tug-of-war as each of my sons drag me in opposite directions, pulling at my heartstrings as well. It's a typical scenario for my four-year old to reluctantly enter any new situation, often studying the scene and all the players—as my younger, three-year old old, bolts into the room, usually hugging everyone he meets and introducing our entire family.

Once my older son settles in, I'm actively pursuing the two of them, with me playing the "monkey in the middle."

Since my boys respond so differently to the changing environments we find ourselves in, I am either preparing my four-year old for transitions or struggling to share expectations with my three-year old in an effort to redirect his energy from getting into everyone and everything.

My husband and I often joke our kids remind us of Jack Klugman and Tony Randall in the show the "Odd Couple." We too wonder if our pair can live together without driving each other (and their parents), "crazy."

The ying and yang of my kids can be traced back to their beginnings: We meticulously planned for Derek's birth, up until his scheduled delivery date. When the time came for Derek to meet the world, he was very reluctant and many complications ensued. When we finally held Derek for the first time, we were, and still are, in awe of his twinkling sky-blue eyes and dusty blond hair. Even though he was constantly pricked and prodded during hospital tests that were performed, both the doctors and nurses echoed what a happy baby he was.

Due to financial obligations, I had to return to my career when Derek was nine months old. My husband drove Derek to and from daycare, which was located in the building next to his office. I was somewhat comforted knowing Derek was close to his Dad—although I must admit—I was a little jealous my husband could visit him throughout the day.

Then, when I discovered I was pregnant again, one month after I returned to my job; I became overwhelmed; I actually had to tell myself to stop thinking about Derek when he was at daycare because I would miss him so much and become too emotional to focus on the tasks at hand. So, as best I could, I tried to move forward, sort of going through the motions with the knowledge I would be changing my lifestyle once the next baby came—even if that meant selling our new house so I could be a stay-at-home mom for a while.

The second pregnancy went by much faster; I often felt as if I was constantly running. I had little time to rest or plan for this baby's arrival. When the time came for Dylan's delivery, the process went much smoother: Once I got through labor, he practically bungi-jumped onto the delivery table, umbilical cord dangling strong.

He had a head full of jet-black hair and almond-shaped hazel eyes. He was a beautiful sight, that is, until someone other than me tried to hold him. In fact, he wouldn't stop screaming for the first six months of life, unless he was in my arms. His pediatrician diagnosed Dylan with colic while my husband described him as "Mr. Grouchy," because he even cried when "Daddy" held him. Although it was challenging carrying Dylan at times, I loved my younger son's desire to be with *only* me. I knew first-hand how quickly babies grew, so I wanted to enjoy this closeness while it lasted.

Understandably, Derek—only a year and a half old at the time his brother came into our lives—was visibly annoyed by Dylan's constant demands and ordered me to put his younger brother "away" so I could play with him like I "use to." It was extremely difficult and often exhausting trying to satisfy my two boys as they vied for my attention, especially the first year after my second son was born—a time when both of them were too young to understand the other had needs, separate from their own.

As my boys second year together began, they started to grow more accepting of each other, although their opposite reactions followed them from home, to school, to outings. During mealtime, my older son tried every food we'd give him, constantly expanding his menu choices. In contrast, his younger brother was reluctant, even suspicious, of trying different flavors.

At the supermarket cashiers struggled to get my older son to say "hello" while my younger son told them everything we bought and where we were going next. When we took trips to the playground, my first-born observed the other kids play before slowly approaching.

His brother, on the other hand, jumped right into whatever the other kids were doing, but louder and faster. I followed him because he took risks, such as diving from the slide like the older kids did, having little regard for his own safety.

Once each son began his quest, he was filled with limitless amounts of energy to keep him going in the opposite direction: one son avoiding something and one attacking it. I was the bedraggled mother, often seen laughing at the comedy of their antics.

Luckily, my younger son, unlike his brother, slept through the night a few months after his birth and continued to do so, affording me some rest. I will always be grateful to him for those extra "zzzzzzzzzzs."

Once my older son was ready for nursery school, I was excited he would have a new place of his own, especially since the preschool he was attending, along with its "stern" Director, was touted as the "best" in our town.

That made it even more devastating when he didn't want to go and pleaded with me not to "drop him off," which was the Director's method for efficiently organizing the students' arrival. Parents were instructed to drive up to the main entrance where teacher aides were waiting to assist the children into the building and to their classrooms. One by one, each car stopped and dropped their child off.

During the beginning days, Derek was one of the few students who didn't want to leave the safety of his vehicle and had to be forcibly lifted away by the most highly revered "Director," who extracted him from the car with her forceful hands before carrying him off. Although I was advised to drive off, as the other carefree families had on their merry way, I agonized for a few minutes before parking my car in the next door lot to watch Derek being carried inside. I felt sick to my stomach as I questioned whether to go into the school to check on him, or listen to the philosophy of the Director, which highlighted the importance of developing independence in toddlers.

I opted for a compromise and instead called the school from my cell phone. The secretary assured me that Derek had settled in "nicely." Still, I wasn't confident he was happy and I worriedly cried. To me, he was still just a baby—a November birthday made him one of the youngest in his class. I knew I would have to make changes, but I wasn't sure what they were. At that moment, I needed to get quiet before the clarity would come.

When I picked Derek up after a few hours, I had to prepare for a struggle of an opposite kind from his younger brother: At dismissal, we were instructed to park our cars and wait on line outside the classroom doors. Once the doors to the school opened, guess who did want to go to nursery school? Dylan would charge the door and push his way into Derek's classroom. The nursery school teachers had to assist me in literally extracting him, as he was kicking and screaming, from his brother's class.

As I left the school those days, with my older son hiding behind my leg—holding on for dear life—and my younger one fighting to get back into the class, I saw many other children happily going to school while their siblings, many who were girls, quietly stood by their mothers' sides. As I passed, a few of the moms curiously stared and whispered as I struggled with my *spirited* (the kind word my twin sister used to describe them when I told her of my woes) toddlers. I knew our school experience wasn't working so I was determined to devise a plan!

I met with the Director, who was feared by many parents, along with Derek's classroom teacher. Although they assured me that Derek was progressing well, I felt uneasy about some of their expectations and teaching methods. For example, I wasn't allowed to enter my son's classroom. Instead, I was permitted to observe the class behind a two-way mirror.

At the conclusion of our meeting, the Director assured me not to worry if Derek, who wasn't fully potty-trained, had an "accident," because she had a surefire cure: She would embarrass him in front of the other kids by keeping him inside during recess. The moment she told me that, my Bronx roots sprouted as I informed her, face to face, she would do no such thing.

As I was leaving the school building I passed Derek coming out of class. He anxiously warned me, "Mommy, you have to go outside 'cause you're not allowed inside our class." Hearing my son say that was the last piece of information I needed to finalize my decision to look for another preschool, a place where Derek could play with less emphasis on rules and structure.

After doing lots of research, I succeeded in finding a class and a director who had a completely different philosophy that focused on play and invited family participation as part of the entire preschool process.

Derek began to flourish and wanted to go to school where he cooked, played outside and drew. It still continued to be a challenge to keep Dylan out of Derek's class, but the teachers were much more helpful, understanding and kind in their approach.

I also realized we needed to create more family harmony and enlisted the help of my husband to deal with some of the challenges we faced on our home front. After making some inquiries, speaking with other parents and educators, and looking at our son's individual needs, my husband and I put some strategies in place and reinforced others that were working.

We made it a priority to follow a schedule for our boys, especially for sleeping, with little deviations as we had previously made for special parties or events. Additionally, we declined invitations to places where our older son could be overwhelmed and our younger son over-stimulated. Instead we channeled their surplus of energy into daily outdoor activities and plenty of exercise.

Since it was difficult for us to eat out, mainly because our younger son would tantrum if he couldn't leave his seat to greet all the patrons or investigate what was in the restaurant's kitchen, we agreed it was easier and less embarrassing to eat our meals at home for the time being.

Once we decided it was time to venture out, we used a proactive approach in gradually teaching our children the rules of dining out. First we frequented the drive-through windows of a few fast food restaurants. We ordered the food and brought it home to eat.

Then we slowly began to go into the restaurants after first ordering the food at the drive-through window. Next, we graduated to a sit down, fancier restaurant by first ordering the food ahead of time so our sons had less of an opportunity to get restless. We did this a few times before actually enjoying the entire restaurant experience together!

No matter where our family went, my husband and I shared a few expectations with our children. If these expectations weren't met, we left. Occasionally we visited unfamiliar places ahead of time to prepare our children and ourselves. When appropriate, we set limits for the time we spent at various outings, so our children gradually became familiar with different places and the accepted behaviors associated with each of them.

Additionally, each son received alone time with both my husband and I to strengthen special bonds. Equally important is providing alone time for my husband and I, which until recently, had been neglected.

As my boys have grown and become more flexible, so has their mother, who celebrates both of her boys' positive characteristics. I treasure each of my son's wonder and uniqueness while also recognizing I am being the best mom I can, especially during challenging times.

My sons have developed their own, special bond since they have grown another year. Each models and balances the strengths of his brother. My older son now encourages his brother to try new foods, and with the help of enhancers such as "ketchup," he is. He also helps with redirecting his younger brother when he's about to get into trouble.

Meanwhile, my younger son aids his sibling by helping him ease into new social situations and partners with him in games and sport's activities. Together they are my Dynamic Duo, coming to each other's rescue!

Recently, our family had a relaxing dinner out—in a "real" restaurant, not a drive-through or fast food joint.

During our meal, the restaurant manager unexpectedly visited our table:

"I am so impressed with how well behaved your children are," he enthusiastically cheered as if in awe. He then shook the boys' hands before inviting us back in the future.

My husband and I grinned at each other with a look only we—as family allies—understood. It's the same smirk we share when Derek tells everyone how much he absolutely loves his new nursery school; and, it's the look my husband and I beam at each other when family, friends and even strangers ask us why Dylan (the "grouch" diagnosed with colic) is always so happy!

It's as if, for the first time on a long traveled journey, we have seen "land" in sight—and what a beautiful vision it is to see our children taking steps forward, our family heading toward the horizon!

I wouldn't trade My Boys, My Joys for anything.

I do, however, sometimes fantasize about seeing some of those mothers from our older son's preschool class in ten years (the ones with the "well behaved" children who watched in disbelief as I struggled with my "spirited" toddlers).

I imagine the moms' harried and bedraggled faces as they attend to their unruly teenagers. The climax of this scenario occurs at the moment their teenagers' tantrums peak and my family enters the scene.

My two "perfectly-behaved" sons gentlemanly strut on by, passing the ranting teens—of course, escorted by their proud, loving mother.

I gleefully wave as I walk past the moms, hand and hand, with **My Boys, My Joys**… into the proverbial sunset…

Reader Reflection

- What is your child's(ren) physical, emotional, social characteristics:
- How are they different from their siblings and/or friends?

LESSON 8

Changing Seasons—
The Rummage Sale: A Lesson in Letting Go!!

Although I feel excited by change, whether it's the seasons or a different place to vacation, I often struggle with adjusting to the varying conditions that accompany it. I still remember those "butterflies" in my stomach during the first month of school, when I was a student and after I became a teacher.

Once I had my own children, my stomach "danced" with excitement, and some melancholy as time and change seemed to move at a sonic pace. Add sleep deprivation into this mix, and many days became blurred into one. While I was thrilled about each of my children's milestones, I sometimes wanted the fast pace of our lives to slow down a little. I learned certain clothes and keepsakes help me hold onto yesterday ….for just a little longer.

Family, friends and even strangers often warned me time would be fleeting when my children were born. I never really understood why I heard this comment so much. Then I realized, until you experience parenting first hand, it's hard to imagine the brevity of each magical moment. To all new moms and dads, please know baby's first few years truly are over in what seems to be a mere blink of the eye—so enjoy them as much as you can!!!!!!!!!!!!!!!!!!!

Changing Seasons
The Rummage Sale: A Lesson in Letting Go!

Every year as the weather changes and a new season is upon us, I procrastinate the sorting and storing of my boys' clothing. "It's such an arduous task"—I mumble to myself—each time I stuff more garments into their already overloaded drawers, all filled with items from last season.

Once I finally begin surveying their inventory, my practical side reassures me my children will be able to fit into these outfits for "just one more year," even though my pragmatic side secretly knows my boys' growth spurt has been constant, so they will most likely be unable to wear much of their previous year's wardrobe. So why do I continue to save their outfits even after they've outgrown them?

The moment I hold my boys' clothes close, pressing them against my cheek, a deep emotional process gets triggered and, I believe, it is the underlying reason I dread the season's end: I am forced to acknowledge my once babies—now three and almost, five—are growing and, like the seasons, constantly changing; worst of all, I have absolutely no control in slowing this natural process.

Their clothing has become one of the few symbols that have helped me visit their first years of life. Ironically, it was their first years—especially all the frenzy given they're only eighteen months a part in age—when I was so sleep deprived and somewhat comatose; I often felt as if I was moving in slow motion. Yet, that span of time now seems to have passed within a few weeks and blinks of an eye. Maybe by holding onto their garments and other tokens, I can hold onto the past for a little longer.

When I heard one of my son's nursery schools was hosting its annual "Rummage Sale," I proclaimed it would be a good time to finally "clean out my closets."

Naturally, I was filled with enthusiasm and ambition as I grabbed and piled their clothes high. This time, prepared with bags and boxes, I browsed over these remnants from our past—organized from smallest to largest in size. Again, once I held them, I was forced to take a stroll down memory lane, a street filled with so many powerful emotions.

I thought, "If these clothes could speak, oh, the memories they would share." The two ivory, woolen sweaters, given to my sons soon after their birth, would boast about how agreeable our boys were when we went to a photo studio to get their first professional picture together. They had to wait over two hours, and still, they were smiling. The denim overalls would giggle remembering how our twosome charged through the pumpkin patch, from a distance appearing as ants running through a maze of orange boulders. And the prim and proper three-piece outfits worn to church events such as Christenings, Communions and

Easter Sundays, would share how unsettling it was when our children, now able to walk (or should I say, run)—and their parents who were chasing after them—couldn't sit still for more than a few minutes in the churches they made a quick and early departure from.

As I remember my boys' expressions during these times and the people we've shared many incredible and beautifully simple moments together, I am both grateful and melancholy. Can I freeze time for just a little longer?

A few days ago, I agreed to meet my husband and my younger son for breakfast at a nearby bagel shop while our older son was at nursery school. When I arrived, I looked into the shop from the outside glass door, just to get a glimpse of my "boys" (including my husband). I was surprised when I saw my husband but couldn't find our younger son, so I searched the small crowd again. After a second glance, I was stunned!

I gasped! The "big boy" right in front of me opening the refrigerator door with one hand and waving to me with the other was MY SON! I watched as he selected his own carton of juice, sat down at the table and began tearing pieces of the buttered-bagel with his teeth.

Like a director, he motioned for me to enter, and as his dutiful mother, I followed his directive—lunging toward him—kissing his sweet cheek and squeezing him so tightly he said, "Mommy, you're hurting me. Please, let go."

I wanted to tell him it's not so easy this "letting go," although I was working on it as part of my growing process as a parent. But my son would have simply grinned as he always does so confident I am wrapped around his little finger (well, not so little anymore). His smirk would widen knowing I am in awe of his total being and the simple joy he experiences in living each moment to its fullest.

As he ravaged another bite of his bagel, still trying to release my tightly woven hands; he looked at me, all the while smiling with his pearly whites, and ordered me to "let go". I gradually let him slip away from my hold, trying to hang on to the moment—like his belongings—like his toddler years—as long as possible.

And, so it was a gradual release when I brought some of my children's belongings, the ones I was able to relinquish, to the Rummage Sale. It was a comforting thought others would benefit from my boys' "stuff" and create new and lasting memories. I know these items are material and fleeting; unlike the timeless and precious moments we have shared as a family.

I was reassured of this when I joined other volunteers for the set-up of the sale. Like Macy's "Preview Day," shoppers, mostly moms, were putting some great "finds" into their piles. There were a lot of tender words as infant and children's outfits were held high in the air while stories were shared. Parents were in wonderful spirits as they donated one of the greatest of all gifts: their time.

While I was organizing some books, I found several I thought my boys would enjoy. I discovered the books had belonged to the children of another mom, who happened to be working next to me. I just met her that day and thought she was one of the sweetest people I've ever spoken with. She graciously shared how much her kids loved reading the stories and how her sister had given the books to her children as gifts. I truly felt honored there was a piece of history being shared between our families. Isn't that what community is all about?

Still, if you happen to unpack or purchase any of my boys' belongings at next year's Rummage Sale, you'll have to wash away the tears. Like sad songs about couples "breaking-up," setting children free to grow-up is *so very* "hard to do."

Reader Reflection

- Was there a moment in time when you realized that your child(ren) was growing too fast?
- Describe the moment and the feelings/memories associated with it.

LESSON 9

Moms Have to Get in the Game Too!
The Making of a Sport's Mom

When my obstetrician secretly told me (my husband wanted to be surprised) I was having a baby boy, I was shocked! I vividly recall sharing the news with a colleague who already had a grown son. As a self-proclaimed "girly-girl," I questioned her, "What will I ever do with a boy?" She immediately responded, "You will love him, that's what you'll do."

BOY—was she right! Once I became the mom of two wondrous sons, the playing field changed; I learned how much I adore watching my athletic and sports—minded twosome gleefully conquer the ball.

Let the games begin!

Remember, whether you were a sports enthusiast or not before having children,—BELIEVE ME— you will become your child's NUMBER ONE fan. In fact, it's so important that you support and

cheer him on when he's succeeding as well as when he's not. Your child will look for you in the stands. Whether he waves to you, shyly smiles or pretends he doesn't see you, he will always know if you are there or not. And he will remember your presence for the rest of his life!!!!!!!!!!!!!!!!

Moms Have to Get in the Game Too!
The Birth of a Sports Mom

As I watch my husband and two sons, five and four, playing catch from the kitchen window that frames my backyard view, a sense of joy settles into my heart. Like a movie created just for me, I am fascinated watching every scene, listening to the muted voices and high-pitched laughter.

My eyes follow their non-verbal cues and daredevil moves, and I hear my voice calling out, "Be careful," as they dive, crash and bounce back onto the rocky lawn. But they can't hear me, and I retreat so as not to spoil their good time with my worry.

It's amazing how much fun they have throwing and racing to "capture" the ball—this awesome trophy to them. And what's so apparent is the unique bond my threesome share as they soar into action, play by play.

This sport's camaraderie is very new to me. Although I enjoyed tag, kickball and chasing the kids on the Bronx streets where I was born, organized team sports weren't a big part of my life. Instead, we entertained ourselves by playing jacks and jumping rope during the day, followed by nighttime water balloon fights and games such as ringing neighbor's doorbells and running.

When I was twelve years old, my parents moved us to the suburbs where I experienced a bit of a culture shock: From streets with no sidewalks—to a school with a "scheduled" gym class—I felt as if I was in a different country. Trying to "fit into" my new environment, I vividly recall the elation I felt when, after many fumbles, I finally succeeded at perfecting my somersault, a gymnastic move we also called a forward roll. When I proclaimed, yelling across to my gym teacher, I mastered my "somersauce," a crowd of teenage onlookers, as well as the coach, were rolling themselves—in laughter.

That night I decided I wouldn't give those kids the opportunity to laugh at *me* again! Determined to perfect my gymnastic abilities, I removed the cushions from our living-room couch to practice what's called a back-bend—a stance I saw some girls doing as a precursor to other, more complicated moves.

For hours I practiced this step of bending backward in an arch, using my arms and legs to balance and support my weight. When I finally mastered this gymnastic move, I was exhilarated beyond belief! When I went to bed that evening, I had visions of nonchalantly displaying my new skill in front of a crowded gym, filled with impressed onlooker, especially those teenagers who had laughed at my last gymnastic feat.

My visions, however, were blurred the next morning when I literally could not get out of bed. My father had to "extract" me with body straight.

Thereafter, I learned and was proud of the many gymnastic skills I perfected; I realized I had to go at my own pace, especially since many of my peers had started practicing when they were only toddlers.

Even though it was unlikely I would become a bona fide gymnast—competing in the Olympics—I discovered, through my efforts, I was a strong and determined person who had the fortitude to achieve her dreams!

So, many years later, I never imagined part of my motherhood role would be to encourage my children to do the same—to be the best they can be—in all they do, including sports. I want to provide opportunities for them to try new experiences and challenge themselves.

To that end, throughout the first few years of their lives, I have introduced and participated with our children in a wonderful array of social, musical and artistic activities. With regard to sports, I've mainly been responsible for gathering brochures and arranging my boys' schedules to coordinate with my husband's limited free time so he can actively participate.

This was especially important last year when my husband, an avid college baseball player and lover of the game, volunteered to coach my older son's T-ball team. Although the focus was on teaching the players the fundamental rules and skills before actually playing a game, I saw the roots of competitiveness sprouting.

Dinner conversations began to focus on our son's "innate" abilities and "rocket" arm. As has been the case in the past, I continued to encourage their camaraderie and pledged to attend as many practices as possible—as a spectator cheering them on.

One afternoon, after I came home from shopping, I saw my husband and boys watching the sport's channel; it was a sight for ***Sports Illustrated*** eyes: Hunched close together on the floor with bowls of popcorn in laps and eyes glued to the set, my presence went unnoticed.

Once the popcorn was finished, I waved a brochure I had picked-up during my travels in front of the television screen they continued to fixate on. The brochure contained information about a local soccer league, and I was compelled to share it.

Surprisingly, soccer was one sport my husband didn't play when he was growing up, so he didn't show a lot of enthusiasm when I suggested our older son might join.

Still, I called the director of the program and arranged for my husband and son to drop-in on a practice, which they soon did. They returned with discouraged looks. Off to the side, my husband said, "Those kids look like professionals; they've been playing since they were two-years old. It's not for him."

After I reminded my son (and his father) about several other activities he'd been unsure of at first and later enjoyed, he agreed to at least try it.

"Would *you* come with me, Mom," he asked. "Daddy always comes to the sports stuff."

"Of course," I immediately responded, although internally hesitant about his request.

The early morning drive to the soccer field was downright scary for this novice sport's mom. I didn't know if I would live up to my son's expectations, especially compared with my husband's participatory role. I never played on any sport's team, and frankly didn't know much about the game.

Once we got to the field, my son said his stomach felt "funny." I told him that I thought he was feeling the "excitement" of the game. Secretly, I too was sick to my stomach, worrying if I placed my son in a situation that would weaken his self-esteem.

I knew he was a newcomer among experienced players—in a competitive environment. Yet, stronger than my fear, was a belief my son would somehow benefit from this challenge.

When I saw the team players, I was impressed at how much sports had changed from when I was a girl. Almost half of the group was female, and they showed some "awesome" moves.

As I watched my son attempt the drills, I knew, as a mother does, he was uneasy. And, as expected, he was somewhat awkward and uncomfortable maneuvering the ball, steps behind the other players.

I didn't realize how difficult it would be to watch my son struggle, but it was; I wanted to rescue him, put him back into baseball, a sport he seemed to have a natural inclination for, one that was easier for him—and easier for me to watch.

Once the drills were completed, a short game followed. Unaware of the rules, my son picked-up the soccer ball and started running down the field. His teammates were calling; "you only kick in soccer; put the ball down."

My son ran off the field towards me. I could see tears welling in his eyes. "Mommy," he pleaded, "Take me home, right now; take me home. I don't like this game."

I hugged my son and so wanted to whisk him away, the

same way I wanted someone to rescue me when everyone laughed at me in gym class. I felt that leaving—making a quick getaway—would be the easiest escape for both of us. Yet, ultimately I knew, running away wouldn't be the best solution for my son—or for his mother.

Instead, I shared some insight with him: I softly explained it would take time to learn the rules of the game and practice the skills, as it did for the other players. I stressed the importance of believing in himself and of becoming a team player who did his best to stay in the game. I reminded him of how wonderful he was doing and that he'd continue to do better. I also promised him, it was his choice whether or not to come back again, after he finished this game.

Just then, a female teammate came over, put her arm around my son's shoulder and invited him back into the game (I could have kissed that girl, offered her my son's future hand in marriage…anything for such a kind deed). Off they went, back to the field!

It was about time I got into the game too! I started cheering my son on, encouraging his moves as I shimmied alongside, following him like a child chasing a precious balloon that was set free.

During a water break, I accosted my son; all "fired-up," I began spewing directives for conquering the ball. It was as if a competitive Locknest Monster, buried deep within, emerged.

"Okay, okay, Mom," he fired back, rolling his eyes at my ridiculousness.

Needless to say, he finished that game and has been going back all season.

My son has improved his soccer skills ten-fold while developing a sense of personal accomplishment and team spirit!

During the last practice the team divided into two groups. My son and his teammates were huddled together planning their strategy, and quicker than I could have imagined, my son scored two goals. Like a superhero, he raised both arms toward the sky.

His teammates patted him on the back, lifted him into the air and hugged him. He wore a smile from ear to ear, and like the soccer trophies he's held for several seasons now, he carried that smile for days.

Next baseball season, this newly evolved "sports-mom" will be accompanying my younger son to T-ball—and who knows what else?

Tennis anyone!

Reader Reflection

- Is there something you never imagined yourself participating in that you now are because you're a mom?
- What does that feel like for you?

LESSON 10

"Specials" Are AWESOME—Everything at Home Is Boring
Scheduling Some Fun!

I was so disappointed when my toddlers told me they were "bored"—even when they were doing what I considered "exciting" activities.

I learned moms may have to trick their children into having fun by changing the appearance of things. Sometimes it helps to call something familiar by a different, more appealing, name—as they do in restaurants: "Polenta" is a fancy name for corn meal. This technique works when planning kid's activities as well and provides a whole new appreciation for what was once taken for granted.

Several toys my children were fascinated with during "play-dates" over some other child's house became common place once I bought them for our home. During conversations with other

moms, they echoed the same scenario. So, using toys and everyday household items in different and creative ways will "spice-up" what was once thought of as routine playtime. Using themes as they do in preschool, such as "beach-day" or "game night" can also provide some very exciting sensory experiences!!!!

"Specials" Are AWESOME— Everything at Home Is Boring
Scheduling Some Fun!

Once I was blessed with my own children, after teaching a classroom of kids for several years, I was confident my sons would experience a world filled with wonder and excitement. To that end, I randomly planned art, music and outdoor activities I "just knew" they would find engaging, and they did—for a while. It was exhausting rummaging through countless books and magazines searching for new ideas using glue, clay, pipe cleaners and the like, plus—trying to find new haunts besides farms and parks to amuse them.

On the home front, I was careful to organize the gamut of toys, which, for several years, filled most of the rooms in our home. Since we couldn't afford to finish our basement, I set-up a play area in an extra bedroom we had. It housed all the amazing toys they owned! I was, however, *amazed* how fascinated my kids were with the toys they found at a friend's house, at nursery schools, or at the store. Yet, once I, or someone else, bought them that same toy, the toy lost its wonder—or rather my boys didn't find the wonder in it. I was disheartened, and found myself echoing my parent's preaching, "Do you know how many kids would love to have all these toys…go all these places…do all these things…."

"We're just bored Mom," my almost five-year old nonchalantly responded, slightly shrugging his shoulders. "Yeah, just bored, Mom," agreed his copycat three and a half year old brother. "I could understand my kids' response if we did nothing," I thought. But, I had invested so much time and energy into providing opportunities for them to experience the world, and they were—"BORED."

As a mother, I felt like a failure. And, I must confess, I was very angry with my children. I mean, I had left what others would consider a successful career, so I could spend quality time with my boys. I thought they would find excitement in all we did. Now, I wondered if it was all for naught.

After a few days of mulling things over and running on auto-pilot between "play-dates" and soccer practice, basically feeling sorry for myself, I knew answers would come…in time.

While cleaning my bathroom (I get a lot of ideas in the bathroom—my one place of solitude—but only when I'm quiet so my kids can't hear me), I read over a plaque I hung several years earlier, before I had my children. The plaque highlights a quote by Ralph Waldo Emerson:

> "Though we travel the world over to find the beautiful
> We must carry it with us, or we will find it not."

After hours of contemplating what this message meant and the meaning for our family, I began to realize we needed to see these wondrous times from a different perspective: like the embossed edging on the plaque, we needed another framework that enhanced the view of our activities. Instead of doing many random tasks, the teacher in me recognized I had to highlight, as a designer does when she puts her unique label on what otherwise would be an ordinary pair of jeans, the excitement of a "typical" day. I also had to help my children pace themselves with a combination of structured and unstructured activities.

My boys had gotten use to always "doing" without a purpose, so when they were still, they were "bored."

We started out by creating a schedule together in their notebooks—including some reading and writing tasks, as well as, self-directed alone time for doing an activity of choice. Immediately, this fostered more direction and independence! I also cleared away all the toys, choosing instead to rotate them—strategically incorporating certain types of toys that helped reinforce whatever they seemed to be interested in at the moment. This way there weren't so many choices.

Next, just as I did in school, I set-up, with the help of my boys, some centers: We placed a bunch of different instruments, some we made and others we purchased, into a large container for our "Music Center"; paints, markers, papers supplies and scrap materials filled our "Art Center"; a kitchen, housekeeping tools, a workbench, blocks and games were in our "Free-Play" area.

The children have loved incorporating center time into their days. Now, when my boys wake-up in the morning, they say, "Hey, let's see what we're going to do today." At first, they were making daily schedules; then, the planning of their day became more internalized, and they didn't need to constantly write down their activities all the time.

Still, we have found preparation is everything, and when my boys disagree on what to do or have new ideas, they create schedules to organize their time. When most of the day runs "on-schedule," then we have more down time for pillow fights, "hide and seek," jumping through puddles or just, as we say "hanging-out."

My younger son recently started a new preschool. When I asked him, "What's the best thing about school?" he responded, "the Specials," which include music; art; gym and library. Again, while in the bathroom, this time in the shower, I had a revelation: "Let's put some 'Specials' into our schedule.

My boys and I cleared the boxes from our unfinished basement. During inclement weather, it's a good place to have "Gym." We lugged their bicycles, scooter, and roller skates inside. We even brought down a boom box, so we could play music while we "rock and roll."

For our "Library," we categorized our books before putting them into some cheap bookcases we bought. We each made our own library card and took turns playing the "librarian." The "librarian" also shares a favorite book during "story-time" and uses a toy scanner to checkout books.

Art and Music often echo whichever holiday is coming as my boys create masterpieces and star in their performances.

What's been most amazing is these activities blend into

each other beautifully and build-upon academic and imaginative-play skills. My boys have even brought old toys into the basement to design a "gas-station" to fix their bikes, and an ice-cream parlor to take a snack-break when they've been on the "road."

Lots of their activities end in science experiments or cooking projects without them even knowing it because it's just plain fun—and I've enjoyed spending time with them, instead of *escaping to the bathroom*, a whole lot more!

Reader Reflection

- Which activities have you enjoyed with your child(ren)?
- Which have you adapted in a new way?

LESSON 11

Playing Hide & Seek Is Fun—
Finding Mom Can Be the Hard Part Once Kids Leave the Nest to Do Their Kindergarten Best.

I discovered going through the stages of early parenting can be as challenging as going through puberty. I never expected to go through so many "Identity Crisis" by the time my children turned five!

After becoming a mom, I often looked in the mirror and saw a woman I didn't recognize. It wasn't so much a physical transformation—although I did look and dress differently. My true metamorphosis was from the inside out since my children had become the focal point of my life. My husband and I felt blessed beyond expression. Still, in devoting my time and person to my children for many years, I suddenly felt lost.

Consequently, I discovered in order to be the best mom, I had to also nurture myself includ-

ing my physical, emotional and spiritual self in order to be an adult role model for my children. Once I learned one transition is followed by another, I became more comfortable with exploring different parts of myself and the world. If new moms learn this earlier than I did, they will be in a much better place!!!!!!!!!!!!!!!!!!!!!!

Playing Hide & Seek Is Fun:
Finding Mom Can Be the Hard Part Once Kids Leave the Nest to Do Their Kindergarten Best.

Just when I settled into motherhood (remember, I'm a slow learner), my first son was about to enter Kindergarten. Again I was struggling with an "identity crisis." I began to wonder, "How many of these will I have to endure during their growing years?"

It's comical when my sons "turn the table" and ask me what I want to be when I grow-up, the same question I, like so many other parents, ask them. Right now they know I am their mommy, but they, in all their infinite wisdom, recognize I have some growing to do and more challenges to conquer. It's only fair they should expect some exciting answers from me. Yet, in contrast to their future desires of becoming a star quarterback or President of the United States, my tentative answers and lists of possibilities seem lame.

When I started answering my children's questions I highlighted the importance of recognizing motherhood as a venerable full-time career, in lieu of, or in addition to, any other professional endeavors women pursue. My curious boys nodded their heads in agreement and then continued asking me about my past and future career aspirations. After I elaborated on my jobs, my younger son advised me; "Mommy you've had *lots* of jobs; you'd better make your mind up soon." My older 5 year-old son, already a bonafide culinary aficionado, was most fascinated I worked at Baskin and Robins while I was in high school. Naturally, he focused on all the ice-cream flavors along with all the creative treats I devoured—ranking this as the best job ever.

After much laughter, I confess to my children, who are both transitioning into half-day school—one nursery, the other Kindergarten, I'm nervous about transitioning myself. I just became comfortable as a full-time mommy after agonizing for months before deciding to take a leave of absence from my teaching position to raise them. I couldn't believe I was facing another crossroads of a different sort: should I get a part-time job during the few hours both my boys will be at school? I recognize my children are becoming more independent, and in the best interest of our entire family, I also need to seek some independence—without worrying if I'll still be a "good" mom.

The truth is: it was easier for me to commit to either motherhood or the pursuit of my career; now, the challenge comes integrating the two: I rationalized a part-time job wouldn't be as overwhelming to manage as my full-time profession was.

To help me decide which direction to turn, I reflected on the thought process I followed when I made the choice to become a full-time homemaker. I discovered I had to review our family's unique priorities, regardless of whatever anyone, even so called "experts," advised. I learned this after feeling like an incompetent failure when I returned to my teaching career the year following Derek's birth. After listening to so many professionals who were balancing home and work, I was blind-sighted when my life became unmanageable and quite harried. I didn't understand why my home and career always seemed to collide, leaving me in a frenzy when I was supposed to be "having it all." I was even more stupefied because teachers often are the envy of many; it's touted as the coveted career by those who want to raise children.

One day while I was at the park on a beautiful summer day, a neighbor with small children like mine, started echoing the same falsities I'd heard from other parents: "teachers have it made; they work half-days, summers off." Although I do concur the time off for holiday and summer vacation is often more conducive to family life than "Corporate America's" schedule, I found myself getting upset and needed to set the record straight on behalf of the majority of hard working teachers.

I, like my colleagues, started planning for the upcoming school year in July, continuing throughout the summer so my lessons were well thought out and relevant. In order to continue the momentum once school started, I had to work a full day planning/teaching and then some. In fact, I didn't leave, nor did most of my colleagues, promptly at dismissal, unless there was a sick child at home, an appointment or a stack of papers to work on later.

Most of the time I stayed after school, often into the early evening before bringing paperwork home with me. Much of the night was devoted to preparing the next day's lesson, grading and/or phone conversations with parents. Meanwhile I tried to rush Derek's dinner, bath and playtime, not to mention time spent organizing Derek's diaper bag for the following morning. Often, I wasn't finished with school work until after 11pm. I recall crying at times when I was in the shower preparing for bedtime and thinking of Derek at daycare the next day.

It was an unexpected surprise for me when I yearned to raise my own children; I knew it wouldn't be fair to my family or my students if I continued to split my time between the two. Most importantly, I was unhappy when I did. After months of rushing around, my husband and I agreed to frugally live on his one salary, even if that meant selling our home. As long as we were able to pay our bills, we'd provide the most stable environment for our boys during their early years, which, for us, meant I'd be home guiding them. We concluded as the kids got older, I'd go back to my career and we could save some money for our future, including their college education. I'm sure a financial advisor would have counseled us differently, but we didn't care.

Choosing to leave my career was one of the biggest and scariest decisions of my life. If that wasn't change enough, I discovered each milestone my children make—each corner they turn—there's a new transition waiting for us

Now, for the first time both my children would be gone for a few hours at school. The thought of extra time during the day set my mind ambitiously wandering to all the different tasks I could pursue. I soon realized the few hours were filled quicker than a gas tank. Any free moments I had as a homemaker, I delved into writing. Like spare change, the little spare time I stored, added up. I was able to publish some local newspaper and magazine articles, along with a few drafts for future children's books.

Since there was little income from my efforts thus far,

the pragmatist in me implemented a back-up plan for finances. I decided to continue writing while also securing a part-time job that provided consistent income. This way I could contribute to the household expenses. It's important to recognize for the several years I've been a homemaker, my husband worked extra to provide while never, not once, urging me to help with the finances. When money was especially scarce, he still didn't advise me to return to my teaching career, which provided a secure salary with full benefits and was close to our home. The knowledge I could always return to teaching was a security blanket, helping to relieve some stress if a position I followed didn't work out.

To implement my back-up plan, I first researched part-time jobs at the schools. Unfortunately, none were available. I was however, contacted to tutor a brother of one of my students. I enjoyed the tutoring, except much of the time invested was on the weekends, instead of while my children were at school.

After several months of searching, I applied for an Educational Advocate position helping children, age birth through five, diagnosed with developmental disabilities, receive educational services. Although I didn't have any direct experience in advocacy, I practiced it in my teaching role on behalf of my students. Another advocate for older children, who I'd be working with, was also hired as part of the grant which funded our salaries. I took this job for several reasons besides the extra money it would provide; it was a way to continue working in education and learn aspects previously unfamiliar to me; and I could schedule my own hours to meet with these families and school districts.

Once I started, I soon realized I was in unchartered waters for sure. By now, I was accustomed to my routine with the children; in contrast, I had to complete my professional tasks around my kid's schedules. It was also the first time I was the least experienced, a trainee turning 39, among so many women who had devoted decades to this profession. At first, it was difficult for me to accept my unfamiliarity and the uncertainty of many advocacy issues. I was comforted when I was able to share my insight as a teacher with coworkers who were unfamiliar with aspects of the educational process.

I recognized another challenge I faced as a part-timer was leaving unfinished work due to time constraints; I learned as much as I could during my scheduled hours, often putting in additional time even if I wasn't getting paid for it. After weeks of devoting extra hours as a way of getting a handle on an overwhelming amount of information, I became better equipped at leaving incomplete tasks for another day so my time with my kids went uninterrupted.

I was lucky to work with a 20 year veteran as a partner. Some cases were new to her as well. Ironically, our boss was initially concerned my partner and I wouldn't get along because we are "so different." We are an amazing team who has been nicknamed the "Thelma & Louise," of educational advocacy, two fair-minded women with the potential of getting tough when educational injustices exist.

My new job provided me with unforeseen professional bonuses: I'm working with grown woman again for an admirable cause while expanding my resume; I look forward to the adult social perks, like drinking a good cup of coffee or mingling at an occasional lunch out; I enjoy the niceties of buying my own trinkets and grooming products to pamper myself and my boys, as well as contributing to paying a small portion of the household bills; I now have a sense of accomplishment!

I even started dressing more professionally again as my husband surprised me with a modern wardrobe to replace outdated clothing, what I sometimes refer to as my "mommywear." My new clothes were the perfect incentive to start an exercise program. Although my efforts so far haven't resulted in a return to my pre-pregnancy weight and shape (which may never happen), I look and feel better than I have in several years, finally reconciling with the notion I'm simply not one of those women whose body bounces back after childbirth.

I'm settling into my new juggling routine at home and luckily finding it doable. After being "Mommy" for several years, I learned to create time for me without feeling as if my boys would suffer. I was able to prioritize my tasks and set boundaries for work.

Prior to having children, my life decisions were definitive, with fewer options. I use to feel uneasy when my choices were grey, instead of black or white. Although I never imagined, at this stage of my life, so many ongoing changes would still persist, I'm learning to navigate in murky waters. Yet, before I remove my goggles, I'm already getting questions about my future plans once both children are in school full day. I'm confident I'll be spending many bedtime hours with eyes wide open, while my husband sleeps soundly, contemplating our future.

Thankfully, I have a few years until I arrive at that crossroad and my next "identity crisis" ensues. It's no wonder I often look in the mirror and marvel, "Who in the world is that woman staring back at ME?"

Reader Reflection

- Do you ever feel as if you are experiencing an identity crisis?
- What do you need to evaluate in order to have clarity regarding which direction to turn?

LESSON 12

Holiday Memories—
"Kitty" and Grandmothers.

Very rapidly, mothers ripen into glorious grandmothers who leave indelible imprints on both their children's and their grandchildren's lives.

I gleefully watch from the sidelines, letting "Granny Lynn" become mere putty in my children's tiny, adoring hands. As she spoils my sons. I often tease and question why I didn't get this "VIP treatment" while I was growing-up?

I believe one of Life's great blessings is:
    A grandma who always has an extra stash of cookies she dotingly saves, eagerly awaiting her grandchildren's visits. Be prepared to see your own mother transform into a grandmother and journey with your children in wondrous ways!!!!!!

Holiday Memories:
"Kitty" and Grandmothers

My mother, now in her sixties, loves being a grandma. After hundreds of requests from my children, she recently agreed to stay overnight. My toddler sons were so excited to have their "Grandma Lynn" to themselves so she could play with them, and especially, read a bedtime story. They heartily laughed when my mother was unable to decipher some of the words without her reading glasses. Both boys eagerly found her spectacles after digging like dogs through her immense and cluttered purse.

But, the biggest hysteria came when they saw their grandma clad in her brightly colored, ruffled pajamas—accented by my father's black socks. After lots more giggling and snuggling, Grandma tucked them in with a promise of "more fun tomorrow."

I was awakened very early the next morning by the sounds of scurrying footsteps and loud whispers—which are my spirited children's attempts to be "quiet." I went to see what all the commotion was and found my two sons hanging over our guest bed, their heads downward, pressed very close to my mother's face. Their hands were covering their mouths, in an attempt to contain their laughter. Grandma Lynn was making a good amount of noise snoring, although she calls it "heavy breathing." Her eyes were half-open—until she jolted up when I joined my sons in their amusement.

"The kids were in here earlier this morning. I must have dozed off again," my mom groggily shared. It was 6:30 am by the time I arrived, so I reprimanded my sons for going into my mother's room so early. Both boys explained they had come back for a second visit because they were very interested in seeing "Grandma's teeth again."

My mother was mortified when she learned my two son's return to her guest room was in response to their discovery of her false teeth sitting in a glass of water beside the bed. My mother is old-fashioned and very private about what she considers "personal," and her teeth or lack thereof falls into this category. Thankfully, after seeing and hearing our laughter, Grandma joined in, now jokingly sliding her teeth in and out of her mouth in a rhythmic pace.

The jesting continued as my sons observed and dissected the contents in the glass as if they were investigating a science experiment. The direct and innocent questions about "where did her real teeth go," "how did she get her teeth out of her mouth if they were glued inside?" were wondrous. My younger, mathematically-inclined son wanted to know if the entire set of teeth cost "more than $100" or did Grandma have to "buy one at a time." The scenario ended with my mother joyfully smiling while hugging my sons—sporting a full set of gums.

I'm often able to use Grandma's teeth to further instruct

my children on the importance of taking care of their pearly whites when they complain, as they sometimes do, I make them brush their teeth too much.

As I watched from the "sidelines," I saw my two boys wondrously playing games starting with "Go Fish" before dragging Grandma outside, tossing a moving basketball to her before returning for a snack inside. Each boy vied for her attention and she didn't disappoint them, bouncing from one activity to the next…until I reminded them Grandma Lynn needed a rest. I could tell my mom was exhausted, yet enamored by all the attention my sons showered her with.

While I continued to watch my boys snuggle with my mom, I knew "Grandma Lynn" would be one of the most important people in their lives; I began to reminisce about my own grandma's visits as a child and how special those moments were, and continue to be, for me.

"Kitty" was a nickname we teasingly called my grandmother as a shortened version of her name: Kathryn. The nickname was very fitting because she was playful and youthful like a kitten. She and my grandfather, a New York City Police Officer, had six children. My grandfather died early, at the age of fifty, leaving my grandmother with some very challenging times ahead of her. One of her first challenges, which she enlisted the help of my father, was learning to drive.

It wasn't long before she was on the road, now able to commute to her new job as a secretary in a religious high school, as well as visit her family scattered throughout the Northeast.

Sometimes when Grandma came, we'd be playing outside with friends as her car passed by. All of us raced home to greet her and taste one of the many delectable cakes and cookies she always brought fresh from, as my mother would say, "the best bakeries in the Bronx."

My friends, upon meeting her, often thought she was an aunt because she didn't look old enough to be a grandma. She probably would attribute her youthful glow to her meticulous hygiene rituals. Whenever Grandma slept over, she would systematically wake early by 5:30a.m., dutifully cleanse her face with a handful of cold cream and rinse it off.

Next, she would turn her head downside and frantically tease her jet-black hair, before swooping and pinning it into a high and tight twist.

Once her grooming was complete we would find her, usually with eyes half-closed, sitting on the living room couch waiting for everyone else to wake-up. She'd often stay a few days doing our favorite things—shopping, talking and eating—before she returned to her own home.

After years of living in the four-bedroom Colonial in Mount Vernon, Westchester, with her youngest daughter (my aunt), they were confronted by robbers one evening after returning home from work. Boldly and brazenly, Grandma ran after them as they took fleet!

Worried about Grandma's safety, my mother had invited her to live with us, as did some of her other children. But, she confided in me she wanted to be independent and not become a burden to her children. Instead, Grandma decided to sell her house and downsize to an apartment.

I was sad when the house that represented some of my earliest Christmas memories was sold. I remember the house sat high above an incline with an entourage of trees;

ironically, most were Christmas evergreen. I vaguely recall an enclosed porch with tiny glass windows. It was on this porch I sat in front of an organ, slamming its keyboard, pretending to be on-stage.

I can still sense the aroma of home cooking from visits I had, and I especially remember eating the best homemade macaroni and cheese I have ever tasted.

As a child, I was scared of the cellar that housed the infamous "cat of nine tails" my grandmother teasingly threatened she would have to take out if we didn't behave well.

Also scary to me as a youngster was a recurring dream I had about roller skating at an uncontrollably fast pace-down the house's precipitous driveway, into oncoming traffic and ultimately down under into a sewer drain gate. On my way down, deeper into darkness, I would abruptly wake-up with heart-racing palpitations.

But the most lasting impressions that still remain with me are those from a Christmas gathering I recall: All Grandma's children and grandchildren were scattered throughout the living room laughing, munching and eagerly awaiting Grandma's cue to sit down for present opening. Grandma enthusiastically put her glasses on before selecting one from many piles of gifts. Once each name on the gift tag was read, the recipient raced to the front of the room and back to his/her place before tearing open their prize.

Every gift I received from my grandmother was wonderful because I felt—even as young as I was—she had spent much time and consideration in her selection, personalizing each present. Her gifts became even more meaningful as I grew older and appreciated their sentimental value.

It was during this Christmas celebration when Grandma gave me a ceramic figurine of "Snow White" with a matching watch clasped at the bottom of its dress; I was enthralled! I wore the watch around my wrist and carefully took it off when I showered and slept. I put the "Snow White" statuette atop a shelf across from my bed so I could see her before I went to sleep each night.

Following Christmas that year, Grandma moved to a quaint, one-bedroom apartment in Park Chester, NY. It was then when different Christmas traditions started and my grandmother earned a new nickname: "Rudolph." Each Christmas season, she traveled to her six children's homes. Her car was the sleigh she maneuvered across the Northeast.

Like the Christmases we celebrated at her home, we continued to eat lots of food and desserts; we started our own tradition: each child in our family took a turn sitting in a designated chair to open presents while we all watched in anticipation. It was as much fun to give as it was to receive. Like a little kid, Grandma's eyes widened as each gift was opened.

During one visit, there was an "Elvis Presley" marathon of movies on television. My grandmother and I, both adoring fans, watched in delight. As the evening progressed, I noticed my grandmother sitting on the couch, eyes closed with head slightly tilted. I could hear her breathing heavily (as my mother does when she sleeps).

"Go to bed, Grandma," I called across the room. When she didn't answer, I giggled and repeated, "Go to bed, Grandma, you've been up since 5:30 this morning. "NOOOoo," Grandma wailed, as she flung her head upright and lifted her feet from the floor, vertically moving her legs in a scissor-like motion:

"I want to watch Elvis," she demanded!

I could not argue with—nor could I ever forget—the endearing and child-like protests she made!

My grandmother died on December 7, 1980, two and a half weeks before Christmas the following year. My family was deeply saddened by her sudden death. We longed for a holiday visit from her.

To our surprise, my aunt delivered presents Grandma had purchased before her death. I felt as if Grandma was watching me as I opened them. Her spirit was with us that year and remains with us—especially during the holiday season.

I often feel as if she is bestowing gifts upon us and guiding our way with her light. Sometimes, when I wake-up in the early morning—when it's still dark out—I feel as if she is sitting on my sofa, waiting for my family to wake-up.

"Snow White" continues to sit high, atop a shelf overlooking my bedroom. The figurine, with its jet-black hair (the color of my grandmas') has aged: some of its smoother surfaces scratched; some of its vibrant color faded.

Yet, like my grandmother, she has matured with dignity and grace, each possessing a beauty that transcends time.

Both Grandma and Snow White represent magical figures in my life and cherished moments from my childhood—moments that become dearer with each visit and every holiday my children share with their "Grandma Lynn."

Reader Reflection

- What's your most powerful memory of your grandmother?
- How has your relationship with your own mother changed now that she's a grandmother?
- What's her relationship with your children like, and what do you cherish about it?

LESSON 13

Evens Verses Odds –
Having Number Three, Looking for a Girl like Me!

No sooner does a mother send her youngest child to Kindergarten, (finally having some alone time), does she contemplate having another baby—even when the "odds" are against her.

I believe so many women are expected to balance a career and a home—with little time for reflection on the life choices they want. Harried moms simply go into autopilot until they realize they're not really moving forward or feeling fulfilled with their lives.

After becoming a stay-at-home mom for several years—shocking many who thought they "knew" me, I adamantly decided I would return to my full-time career once my children were ready for kindergarten. I didn't imagine my inner longings truly included having another baby, a girl for me to share my womanhood with. The dilemma

I encountered was I turned 40 and questioned, along with others in my inner circle, whether that would be the best choice for our family. My husband and I decided to contemplate the possibility for now, rather than make a definitive choice. I am proof you never know what your feelings will be once you experience motherhood, so be prepared to surprise yourself!!!!!!!!!!!!!!!!

Evens Verses Odds:
Having Number Three Looking for a Girl like Me!

Lately I've been toying with the idea of having another baby, although my practical side, and that of my husbands', does not want me to even entertain this thought for several reasons. I'm at an age, well, let's say—when I don't have too many more childrearing years left. And although I've been blessed in getting pregnant easily, I have been sick throughout my pregnancies followed by "challenging" deliveries.

Additionally, I'm exhausted just thinking about more sleepless nights, the rigors of breastfeeding, frequent pediatrician visits—all the while trying to keep up with my two spirited and active boys.

It's been unfortunate we don't have any family close by to help, at least with giving my husband and I an occasional break. And it's been challenging finding a competent and trustworthy babysitter who I feel comfortable leaving my children with so I can pursue my writing more and have a monthly dinner out with my husband.

So it wasn't a surprise when I didn't receive too much support—except from my two sons who have cheered me on and even volunteered to help with a new sibling the few times I hinted about my desire to "possibly" have another baby. A close friend, who doesn't have any children but is very loving to mine, as well as supportive of my challenges, told me she has concerns about the stress another baby would bring into our already harried lives.

When our boys were three and four, my husband reminded me we were just starting to have a little time alone since our children had become less dependent with dressing and feeding, and both boys were potty-trained. Additionally, when the mood strikes them, our boys have grown to play alone together, although it usually looks like wrestling or tackling.

As they've matured another year—with Kindergarten around the corner, I'm again filled with thoughts of a third child. This time I was compelled to share my thoughts with other mothers I know. As expected, I received mixed reviews. Although a few moms I've met have been more encouraging, others have warned, with a third child, one is always "left out." Or, I've often heard, "that's why you only have two hands—one for each child. A third puts you over the edge."

After these brief discussions, I often feel torn: My pragmatic voice screams, "Are you crazy even thinking about having another baby?" My emotional side retorts, "Stop analyzing your feelings and just follow your heart!"

When I see a pregnant woman or hear of a friend's upcoming "delivery date," I occasionally sense a vacuous ache in my belly. Or, I may see a mother with an infant, and become filled with joy; my heart opens to the baby like a bud drawn toward the light of the sun.

When I receive store catalogues, I still browse through all the infant sections imagining which items I, now a discerned Mommy, would buy first, along with other new gadgets I wish I had when my two boys were born. When I visit the book stores, I'm drawn to the "Baby" section where all the "name" books adorn the shelves: Certain names call out to me, and I have narrowed my list to a few choices should I ever have "number three."

I realize I need to, as I have in the past with other life transforming decisions, get quiet and listen to that internal voice of truth (and consider that of my husbands'). In order to uncover my decision I have to confront some of my inner turmoil, analyze my motivation and answer some tough questions that may be impacting my strong desire to procreate:

Am I scared of my boys growing-up too quickly? Am I having a difficult time "letting go," so I want another baby? Will having another infant help me feel as if I'm younger so I can avoid dealing with aging as well as another "identity crisis?" What impact will another child have on the lives of my two wondrous boys who already occupy so much of my time?

Additionally, deep down, on a visceral level, I am still mourning the miscarriage I had before my first son was born; I lost the baby during the second trimester, very unexpectedly. My husband and I were devastated, and although we grieved and I sought counseling, we will always carry the loss with us.

Sometimes I wake in the middle of the night startled by a recurrent dream I have: my baby who I miscarried is telling me to have another baby girl. Other times, I awaken with an awareness of a far-off voice imparting wisdom, echoing that my life is happy as it is, and I'm too old to go through the pregnancy, as well as the first few sleep-deprived years of waking and feedings.

Yet, I often wonder how having a daughter would change my life. I never imagined having sons—My Boys, My Joys—would be so life transforming! I love them beyond comprehension and thank God I have them, and they have each other!! If I were to become pregnant again and give birth to another boy, my twosome is the reason I would be ecstatic!

Still, there's this little niche inside my heart to nurture a baby girl and experience mothering her. Certainly, with a girl, I would probably go shopping a lot more, which I love and did from a very young age with my own mother. Just go into any children's store and compare the huge amount of space the girls' clothes occupy with the tiny section allocated for boys' attire. Unlike my boys, I love the colors pink and purple and lots of the "girly" dolls and games.

But, most importantly, I would love to have a daughter to share my womanhood with; to help her grow in ways and have opportunities I never did, including those found in sports—something my boys have enlightened me about. I have a special mother and son bond with each of my boys, and would like to have one with my daughter—as I do with my own mother.

My mother calls me every day, and I have gotten closer to her as we've grown together. I can tell her things and share experiences unique to our mother/daughter relationship.

But time will tell. I could have another boy if we decide to get pregnant, and I don't want him to feel as if we are disappointed; who knows, I may have to wait for a granddaughter to see pink in my home.

Sometimes when trying to answer life-changing questions, such as whether to have another child, a simple moment in a day can change perspective or provide crystal clear clarity.

As of right now, I'm still in opaque. But, if you see a 40-year-old, queasy, pregnant woman, chasing after two amazing boys, it might be me.

Look a little closer, and I'm sure you'll see a little grin, and, of course, the "glow."

Reader Reflection

- Once your child(ren) is ready for school, what are you ready to pursue?
- Are you surprised by any longings for more children, or has an unexpected turn in your life caused you to change directions?

Postscript

It is my intention and desire to follow *MommyBest...Book 1* with a sequel, *Book 2* for lessons I have learned as my boys grow from age five through age thirteen. I wish someone had shared their experiences regarding the evolution of the mother and son relationship and the ways in which moms will feel as if they are in a different land, looking toward a new horizon. There are vast contrasts between the first and second five years plus of my boys' lives. Stories dealing with holidays, relatives, friends, Dad's new role, sports competitions, birthday parties, family time, and vacations will convey wondrous insight, and hopefully a few laughs. I'm also including helpful ways of dealing with school issues including, teacher conferences, class moms, the PTA and riding the school bus. *MommyBest...Book 2* will highlight those years from five through thirteen that help shape the future of your children, yourself and your family before those "dreaded" teen years, which will be covered in *Book 3*, with your good graces.

The journey is constant and the surprises are magical moments in time. I look forward to all of you growing and enjoying life, as we are, together as a family! I thank you for letting us share our trip with you and we'll see you at the next stop!!

BOOK ORDER INFORMATION

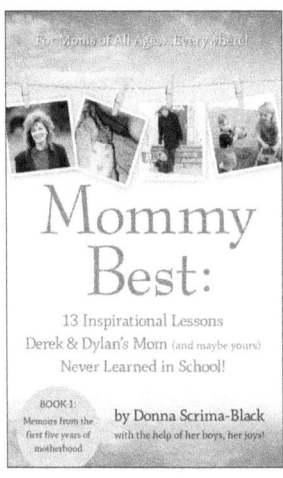

MommyBest:
13 Inspirational Lessons Derek & Dylan's Mom (and maybe yours) Never Learned in School

BOOK 1
Memoirs from the first five years of motherhood.

Orders may be placed at our website:
Mommybestbook.com

Bulk quantities may be ordered by:

~Individuals, Organizations, Hospitals (especially those with maternity wings/ Lamaze classes)

~Any group devoted to:

- The recognition of women's achievements
- The celebration of motherhood in all its splendor and struggle
- The support of women's advocacy issues.

www.ingramcontent.com/pod-product-compliance
Lightning Source LLC
LaVergne TN
LVHW051121080426
835510LV00018B/2174